MATTERS
OF VITAL
INTEREST

MATTERS OF VITAL INTEREST

A Forty-Year Friendship with
Leonard Cohen

ERIC LERNER

DA CAPO PRESS

Da Capo Press
Hachette Book Group
1290 Avenue of the Americas, New York, NY 10104
www.dacapopress.com

@DaCapoPress; @DaCapoPR

Printed in the United States of America

First Edition: October 2018

Published by Da Capo Press, an imprint of Perseus Books, LLC, a subsidiary of Hachette Book Group, Inc. The Da Capo Press name and logo is a trademark of the Hachette Book Group.

The Hachette Speakers Bureau provides a wide range of authors for speaking events. To find out more, go to www.hachettespeakersbureau.com or call (866) 376-6591.

The publisher is not responsible for websites (or their content) that are not owned by the publisher.

PRINT BOOK INTERIOR DESIGN BY JEFF WILLIAMS

Library of Congress Cataloging-in-Publication Data
Names: Lerner, Eric, author.
Title: Matters of vital interest: a forty-year friendship with Leonard Cohen / Eric Lerner.
Description: First edition. | New York, NY: Da Capo Press, 2018.
Identifiers: LCCN 2018007895| ISBN 9780306902703 (hardcover) | ISBN 9780306902710 (ebook)
Subjects: LCSH: Cohen, Leonard, 1934-2016. | Lerner, Eric. | Composers—Canada—Biography. | Singers—Canada—Biography. | Buddhists—Biography.
Classification: LCC ML410.C734 L48 2018 | DDC 782.42164092/2 [B]—dc23
LC record available at https://lccn.loc.gov/2018007895

ISBNs: 978-0-306-90270-3 (hardcover), 978-0-306-90271-0 (ebook)

LSC-C

10 9 8 7 6 5 4 3 2 1

CONTENTS

For all the kids

one

ROSHI

SAINT JOSEPH'S ABBEY IN Spencer, Massachusetts, is a magnificent complex of fieldstone buildings surrounded by rolling acres of working farmland, a monastery of the Catholic Cistercian Order of the Strict Observance, whose monks, popularly known as Trappists, live a cloistered life of prayer and contemplation. In the 1970s some of the more eclectic members of the order invited the Japanese-born Rinzai Zen master Joshu Sasaki Roshi to visit the abbey once a year and lead them in an intensive Zen retreat known as *sesshin.*

Joshu Sasaki Roshi came to America in 1962, dispatched by his superiors at a prestigious temple in Japan—some later said it was to get rid of the troublemaker—in response to a request for a teacher from a small group of Southern California Zen enthusiasts. He arrived speaking no English, carrying a beat-up old Japanese-English dictionary. His supporters established Cimarron Zen Center a few years later in a dicey part of Los Angeles not far from the scene of the 1965 Watts riots. In 1971 the group purchased an old Boy Scout camp about an hour east of the city, high up an eight-thousand-foot mountain. The Mt. Baldy Zen Center was intended to re-create the atmosphere and training practice of a traditional Japanese Rinzai Zen monastery.

Rinzai is a distinct "school" of Zen, which is a distinct school of Buddhism. In its formal practice, Rinzai demands the precise execution of every ritualized group activity. Students wear identical black Zen robes and sit in meditation—*zazen*—in the zendo, the meditation hall, on identical black mats and cushions facing each other in parallel rows, everyone maintaining the identical meditation posture: spine erect, legs in half or full lotus, hands cupped with the thumb tips touching at the top of an open circle held above your navel, never dropping into your lap. Head is tilted slightly down. Eyes are half open, focused on a spot on the floor in front of you, never, ever wandering, especially in the direction of anyone else. Once zazen commences there is no moving, no sniffling, no coughing. Any infraction is subject to the immediate disapproval of the officer of the zendo—the *jikijitsu*—who periodically shouts: *No moving! Quiet!*

At times he prowls the zendo carrying a polished flat wooden stick, elbows flared like a samurai swordsman's, as if daring a student to nod off or let his hands fall. Then he pounces, lightly tap-tapping the shoulder of the miscreant. Mutual bows precede the famous Rinzai whacking with the stick. The chastised student bows again in thanks. The jikijitsu stalks on.

Walking meditation is similarly choreographed: hurry up in lockstep, hands held tightly chest-high, a long, black caterpillar marching around outside the zendo no matter the weather. Group meals in their exacting formality of silent bows and hand gestures are no break at all from the intense concentration on not fucking up. The purpose of all this, along with the sleep deprivation, is to induce a profound desperation that convinces you to launch some kind of kamikaze attack on your ego.

It is not Mindfulness for Corporate Advancement or a form of stress reduction. It's not supposed to make you feel particularly better until you break through in an instantaneous flash of enlightenment.

Satori.

At any rate, that's the hype.

~

Summoned by the rhythmic sound of heavy wooden clappers—slow and ominous at first to grab your attention, then steadily increasing in tempo to cause panic—the Zen

students filed into the makeshift zendo, a carpeted reception room of the abbey repurposed for this "informal"
session. I was among the half dozen first-time students
stumbling at the doorway to make sure we correctly exe-
cuted our newly learned bows before finding our places,
bowing again, and getting into zazen posture as the sesshin commenced. It was April 1977.

I didn't realize that the spot I'd claimed next to the
window was directly opposite the jikijitsu, the zendo leader,
until I noticed the low table placed beside the empty cush-
ion with a bell, an incense holder, and a lighter. I heard
footsteps descending the stairway behind me. Keeping my
head down as instructed, I stared at his bare feet. His lower
body dropped into the frame of my vision. I could see his
hands make sharp, sweeping movements as he snapped
the hem of his robe over his knees and tucked it under his
feet, turning himself into an impressive black pyramid. I
lifted my gaze surreptitiously to glimpse his face.

It was Leonard Cohen.

Really?

His was a famous face, prominently displayed on the
cover of his first record album that everyone owned in
1968, his thick helmet of black hair hanging practically
to his dark brows over eyes with sparkles of light staring
at you, the Semitic nose protruding over curious curved
lips in a pose reminiscent of a nineteenth-century French
poet. I'd heard nothing new from him since his second

album in 1969, the one with the white cover and "Bird on the Wire" on it. I had no idea what he'd been doing since, but his face was older, tighter, leaner and more purposeful.

The zendo leader is supposed to act as if he's not even breaking a sweat during the day's arduous schedule to make everyone else feel even worse. Leonard sported a look of placid, resigned indifference, even when his feet fell asleep and he struggled to rise to lead the group out of the zendo for the regimented walks. His robes looked as if they'd been pressed each morning, and his white collar remained crisp and spotless for the entire week.

By the fifth day, the effluvium of tortured minds and bodies suffocated the zendo. After lunch there was a break for showers, a short nap, or wandering around outside contemplating your predicament. I'd found a little path that led to an isolated area behind the main building where I could be alone. I rounded the corner to my spot. Leonard was up ahead, smoking a cigarette in a stately posture, one hand supporting the elbow of the hand that held his cigarette. I was about to go back and leave him alone, but he turned toward me and shrugged: *It's okay, no need to split.*

I sat down on the fieldstone wall and gazed out at the rolling farmland, glancing occasionally at him. He continued to smoke and seemed to be deeply considering some matter with furrowed brow. I knew nothing then of his life, and since I was twenty-seven at the time, even less about the life of a forty-two-year-old man.

He finished his cigarette and stubbed it out on the ground before neatly depositing the butt in the big cuff of his robe. I could hear his huge sigh from where I was sitting. I got up to return to the zendo. He turned and we stared at each other. His serious face pantomimed bewilderment. I smiled at his silent question: *What in the world are a couple of smart Jewish boys like us doing here?*

Thirty-five years later, while I was working on a novel fashioned as a biography of a fictional New Age teacher, I reread the books that originally sent me careening down the spiritual path, dropping out of Harvard in 1969 to make an overland pilgrimage to India. The book that resonated most strongly now was *The Varieties of Religious Experience*, written in 1902 by the founder of modern psychology, William James.

I asked Leonard if he'd ever read it.

"Of course. But I can't recall a word. Does it shed any light on our predicament?"

"Listen to this." We often read stuff to each other over the phone.

"According to James, *there is a marked contrast between the two ways of looking at life, between those we call the healthy-minded, who need to be born only once, and the sick souls who must be twice-born in order to be happy.*"

"Twice-born, eh?" He never lost that Canadianism. I think it has infected my own speech. "That's pretty good."

I went on. "*The healthy-minded temperament has a constitutional incapacity for prolonged suffering, and its tendency to see things optimistically is like a water of crystallization in which the individual's character is set.*"

"I used to be one of those guys, y'know?" he offered.

"Really? When?"

"Playing upstairs in my bedroom with my chemistry set at the age of twelve. Then I wandered into the fog of sexual desire from whence I've yet to fully emerge."

"I know what you mean."

"Of course you do."

"Here's the best part," I went on. "James says the twice-born *have a more morbid way of looking at the situation. It is as if there were in their human consciousness a feeling of objective presence, a perception of what we may call:* something there *more deep and general than any of the special and particular senses by which the current psychology supposes existent realities.*

"*The psychological basis of this twice-born character seems to be a certain discordancy or heterogeneity in the native temperament of the subject, an incompletely unified moral and intellectual constitution.*"

"That's not a bad description of IT."

Some years before, Leonard had named the peculiar and particular condition that ailed us: *IT*. After much consideration, we agreed that IT had little to do with clinical depression or even a neurotic disposition. We weren't inherently dark souls (he had a hard time contradicting this popular misconception), nor were we stubborn refuseniks of happiness. Rather, as William James perfectly described, we possessed some feeling of an internal presence that contradicted what the allegedly healthy-minded perceive and feel.

To us IT was a certainty not an uncertainty, a certainty that there is something ineffable yet more real in the universe than anything we could touch, taste, or fuck, a certainty we could not dispute no matter how hard we tried. IT was a spectral, brooding presence at the half-open doorway, an incessant reminder that we could not dwell in any provisional refuge, because in these ill-furnished, meager huts our lives could only be lived *as if,* pretending that the paper-thin scrim we hid behind was reality, while the presence at the half-open door mocked our beliefs, mocked the drugs we ingested to silence it, mocked the cum we spent trying to drown it, even mocked the applause we sought to dissolve the bewildering anguish, the feeling of loss for what we'd never possessed.

"Does the good Dr. James prescribe a cure for our malady?" Leonard asked.

"Get this. He says the twice-born *must experience religion . . . not as a dull habit, but rather as an acute fever.*"

"I was hoping he prescribed beautiful young women."

∿

I met Joshu Sasaki Roshi at the same time I met Leonard at that sesshin at Saint Joseph's Abbey in 1977. Roshi is very short, almost as wide as he is high. At 107, the last time I saw him shortly before he died, his cheeks and shaven head were as smooth and soft as they were when I met him at seventy. His face is on acid. Really. It's not your mind that is tripping. His face morphs in an instant from an expression of distant communion with the cosmos to bored but kindly attentiveness to you, and it changes just as fast to an expression of adamant certainty when he insists you must comprehend what he's telling you.

He wears impeccable white robes that emit a whiff of fresh laundering. He sits on a slightly raised platform holding a small curved stick of polished hardwood that you try not to notice, much less stare at, because you're trying not to stare at anything, even though there are all kinds of interesting things to check out in the room, all kinds of distractions, and he's the biggest distraction of all, but you are resolved not to be distracted from the reason you're kneeling before him, the reason you've spent the past three hours deep in zazen.

This is *sanzen*, the meeting with the master.

How do you realize your true nature when you are looking at the pine tree?

Say what?

As far as I know he gave this first koan to everyone, though I'm sure there are exceptions and contradictions to all the facts about him I'm presenting.

Roshi's English left much to be desired. He repeated the koan again slowly, his eyes nearly closed, enunciating each word with an apologetic smile that I would learn was really a wickedly sarcastic denial that he might ever apologize for anything. Nevertheless, the purpose of this first encounter on the first morning of the sesshin was for me to at least get the words of my first koan right. I nodded, indicating that I understood what he'd said.

Then he opened his eyes and asked my name and repeated it. *Elic.* He almost never forgot a student's name. That was the end of the small talk. He looked at me in the expectant way all teachers do after posing a question, as if this one was on a par with, say, *Who was the second president of the United States?*

Even though I wanted further clarification about which pine tree in particular he was referring to, I intuited that anything I might ask would be a lame gesture on my part.

"True nature," he surprised me, breaking the silence. His eyebrows, weird little black birdwings that clung to his forehead, rustled and his eyes opened wide, struck by inspiration. He leaned toward me: *Psst, I'm gonna tell you a secret.*

I rose from my heels as he intoned, "True nature same as Buddha nature. Same as true self." He seemed pleased, as if he'd never put it exactly that way before, which of course was nonsense; he'd probably said the same thing a thousand times.

But it was our little secret.

Then he reached for his small bell and rang it softly. Our meeting was officially over. I prostrated with upraised palms, got up, backed away, bowed again, and left. I was excited because it's always exciting when someone tells you a secret. You feel special for the confidence, even if someone revealed they have cancer. The downside to a secret is that you're dying to tell someone. I'm exuberant by nature and not good at keeping secrets. The problem was that this was only the first day of a week of silence, and besides, sanzen is a strictly private encounter akin to the Catholic confessional.

I returned to the zendo, unable to entirely wipe the giddy smile from my face. As I sat down and folded my legs, I was aware that Leonard was glancing at me inquisitively. I gave him a small nod to indicate that I felt our time spent in this enterprise was indeed time well spent. He seemed pleased.

∾

"Ah, Elic. Hai. Koan." Roshi greets me. We meet four times a day in sesshin.

Eric replies, "How do I realize my true nature when I'm looking at the pine tree?"

"How DO you realize true nature when looking at the pine tree?" Roshi demands.

I am still clueless.

Roshi turns his head slowly and looks up. He is look-ing at a pine tree, demonstrating to me how to realize your true nature when you're looking at the pine tree.

For the next six days Roshi pantomimes his interest and awe in his imaginary pine tree. He repeats, sometimes with irritated impatience, that my true nature is the same as Buddha nature, the same as true self.

During my last sanzen on the last day of the sesshin, I am practically falling asleep in front of him. Roshi once again looks at his imaginary pine tree, but this time he isn't pantomiming. Roshi is realizing his true nature as he looks at the pine tree in the sanzen room.

Zap.

I catch a glimpse, inhale a whiff, and feel the breeze of true nature across my face.

I return to the zendo. Leonard stares at me. I nod. He seems relieved.

⁓

Roshi, Leonard, and I were quite drunk, lying in triangu-lar proximity on the floor of the thickly carpeted upstairs room, recently the inner sanctum of realizing true nature but now the scene of an equally important ritual of Sasaki Roshi's—imbibing cognac. Leonard had casually invited me to join the party after the sesshin ended that after-noon. Old students dropped by to thank Roshi, present-ing him with gift-wrapped bottles and having a glass with him. Now only the three of us were left; four, counting Roshi's translator who was passed out in a corner.

I was thrilled, not just for my intimate proximity to the master, but also for the revelation that we both loved alcohol!

In the fall of 1973 I'd flown to Mumbai, India, to practice Buddhist Vipassana meditation as taught by S. N. Goenka. I went on to meditate with his teachers in Rangoon, Burma, and then I spent time in a rural monastery in Sri Lanka. I returned to America riding a swelling wave of interest in the teachings of Eastern gurus and masters and the versions taught by their young Western acolytes who had studied with them.

I gave short shrift to every other method, ism, and practice than the one I embraced. Unable to contain my enthusiasm, at the tender age of twenty-six I wrote a spiritual memoir: *Journey of Insight Meditation: A Personal Experience of the Buddha's Way.* Despite its clunky title, it was warmly received in the burgeoning world of the New Age spiritual awakening.

I tried to be a good old-school Buddhist. I gave it my best shot for several years, adhering to the Dharma, plodding along its precise Path of Purification with its Four Noble Truths, Eightfold Noble Path, and exacting enumeration of all the things you must do and refrain from doing. It's more like a ladder than a path, up up up or down down down in the endless cycle of birth and death and rebirth, as you rise to or backslide from your goal of Nirvana, the cessation of these endless rebirths.

Freedom!

I'd returned to America, Land of Freedom and Home of the Brave, and I was going to be free and free my countrymen. George Washington Buddha!

I probably could have joined Joseph Goldstein and Jack Kornfield and a host of others whom I'd come to know well and assumed the mantle of an American Teacher of Buddhism. It was a good gig in a growth industry.

"More cognac, man?" Leonard held out the bottle, not as a question but a prompt for me to lift my empty glass so he could get a better angle to refill it. Roshi gestured for him to keep pouring. I was impressed by Leonard's steady hand. We all raised our full glasses and Roshi explained the salutary properties of cognac in barely comprehensible Japlish. Then we toasted Leonard.

"Mmmmm." Roshi wiped his lips with the back of his hand.

If I'd still been a Buddhist, for this blatant transgression of various rules and regulations pertaining to inebriation and mental foggery I was risking rebirth as a salamander in my next life.

Reincarnation. Tibetan fairy tale. Roshi told me a few years later.

"Let's try this one. Roshi likes Courvoisier but I find it a bit sweet." Leonard held up a new bottle, Rémy Martin,

which I'd never heard of before. My education was proceeding by leaps and bounds. Roshi was lying on his side,
balancing his round body on some point of the sphere
where his hip might have been, anchored by his chin resting on one hand, elbow planted in the soft carpet, leaving the other arm holding his glass free to direct activities
without spilling a drop.

This is no tale of the magical powers of a master, only
an account of a really impeccable drinker, which had always been one of my aspirations in life since I'd begun the
activity in earnest at fourteen.

Roshi sussed out that Leonard was touting the virtues of Rémy, so he picked up a new bottle of Courvoisier
that had enough *X*'s and *O*'s on the label to play tic-tac-
toe. We held a lengthy tasting. I preferred the Rémy, but
Roshi denigrated my preference. Was he calling me a
pussy in Japanese?

~

Earlier that day, at the group's final gathering, Roshi's
translator announced that since this was an "informal sesshin," Roshi would answer questions regarding "the practice of Buddhism." I was looking forward to it. He'd yet to
say a word about Buddhism. I had my question ready.

"Roshi, we've been here a week and you've never once
mentioned *sila*. Why is that?" It was admittedly pretentious
on my part, using the ancient term for "right conduct."

After my first pilgrimage to India in 1969 ended with a failed hashish-smuggling scheme hatched in Teheran, I returned to Harvard and changed my major from History and Literature to Sanskrit and Indian Studies.

Roshi listened with his make-believe interested face as the translator relayed my question to him in Japanese. Then—and I swear I'm not making this up—he stared at me across the room, and his right hand darted out and slapped his forehead. With great satisfaction he removed a squashed mosquito that had been buzzing in his proximity, a heinous breach of right conduct if ever there was one. Roshi seemed unperturbed by the implications of his action for his future rebirths and proceeded to answer my question. In translation it went something like this:

"You are a baby in a big body. And you have a very big head with a big brain. Don't ask me what to do. Figure it out yourself."

≈

The three of us were lying on our backs beside three empty bottles of cognac. Perfect symmetry. Somehow Roshi found another bottle and roused everyone for yet another toast. Leonard and I obediently held up our glasses as Roshi poured. My tongue was numb.

"Not bad, eh?" Leonard turned to me.

When I met him in 1977, Leonard was already intent on keeping his private life as far removed from the limelight of his career as possible. He cultivated a semi-mysterious persona for the stage and interviews and lived outside the music scene, or any scene for that matter. Only a few of his friends even knew about his relationship to Sasaki Roshi, much less that he had moved to Los Angeles from Montreal not for the music business, but for Roshi.

Leonard considered himself part of history's long lineage of serious poets. He'd achieved early success in that regard in his native Canada, and as a literary novelist as well—*Beautiful Losers* is a fantastic read—but his aggregate audience amounted to only a few thousand. Until he picked up a guitar.

"To get girls," he told me, half joking, on several occasions. Leonard Cohen, scion of a prominent, highly respected old Jewish family of Montreal, never believed any of the hype of the sixties. He wore a suit and tie—he was an early Armani adapter—not as an Elvis Costello–like costume, but because he was a graceful man of impeccable old-world manners who wasn't rebelling against anything.

His intense involvement with Sasaki Roshi presented a delicate situation for him. Leonard was keenly aware that his participation in a New Age religion could be publicly embarrassing. At that time Allen Ginsberg and other poets and artists were embracing the brilliant Tibetan teacher Chögyam Trungpa Rinpoche, but Leonard wasn't Ginsberg, who loudly, joyously exhorted the world to come and join him. Even though other noted poets had their

Zen connections, Leonard didn't want to talk about his. Newly religious enthusiasts of all stripes always sounded a bit foolish to him. It wasn't until twenty years later that he spoke about Roshi publicly, and even then elliptically, despite Roshi's profound and enduring influence on his life. I didn't know it that evening, lying on the floor with the two of them, but Roshi would have that effect on me as well.

"Elic."

Leonard poked me out of a brief doze-off. Realizing that Roshi was addressing me, I managed to sit up. Was sanzen about to begin? Was Roshi going to embarrass me by demanding I answer my koan in front of Leonard?

"Yes, Roshi?" I managed.

"You come to Mt. Baldy."

I squinted at him. Was this my new koan?

He squinted back, imitating me, until I understood it was neither a koan nor an invitation, but simply a statement of fact.

"Sure."

two

NEANDERTHALS

"Ooooooooooooold Eric?"

"Ooooold Leonard," I responded to his greeting on the phone.

He wasn't that old when he'd anointed himself Old Leonard, nor was I when he added the honorific to my name, but over the years the fifteen-year difference in our ages kept shrinking until now, some thirty-five years after we first met, we'd become, in our minds at least, two old guys.

We spoke only on landlines. If I was out when he called, he'd leave a baritone parody of his singing voice on my voice mail: *It's Ooooooooooooooooooold Leonard. Speak to you later, man.*

"How are you doing?" he inquired with mock good cheer.

"Not bad. Yourself?"

"I can't complain. Wait a sec. I'm going to pour myself another cup of coffee. Don't go anywhere."

I heard him put the phone down on the table while he rattled around in the kitchen.

"Here we are again. What a lovely day outside. It's terrific!" he declared, like one of those shipwrecked guys in a *New Yorker* cartoon, washed ashore on a patch of sand with a single scraggly palm tree, surveying the vast empty ocean surrounding him to the horizon: *It's terrific!*

I knew he was sitting at the small antique pine table, distressed like us, tucked into the little nook formed by the tiled island beside the sink in the kitchen in the top-floor apartment—identical to the one downstairs—of the duplex in Los Angeles we purchased back in the summer of 1979. At the time its most attractive feature besides the price was its proximity to Roshi's Cimarron Zen Center, a ten-minute drive away. We would always refer to the house by the name of the street it was on: *Tremaine*.

In those early years when I came upstairs for coffee and conversation Leonard insisted I take "the best seat in the house," at the table beside the second-floor window, with the chair turned sideways, looking out at our deceptively placid neighborhood of old Spanish stucco houses, the jacaranda trees blooming delicate purple in the spring, the calm tableau regularly shattered by hovering police helicopters pursuing fleeing suspects through the alleyways. We quickly installed security doors and bars on the windows in imitation of our neighbors.

I moved out of Tremaine seven years later, first to Malibu, and then back east to Northampton, Massachusetts, but the best seat in the house awaited whenever I came into town to toil in the movie business and stayed with him. In the cool early mornings I'd walk up the back stairs and we'd sit at the table over coffee and toast and begin a conversation that we often picked up again after our respective day's labors, conversation that lasted until well after midnight.

Unless he was out of the country, we usually spoke on the phone once a week for an hour or more, bringing each other up to date on the latest crises of wives, children, careers, lawsuits, health, or some toxic combination of the above, before proceeding with our forty-year joint inquiry into what we termed *matters of vital interest.*

"Check this out," I announced over the phone that morning in the spring of 2013.

"I'm all ears, bro."

Once, I would have heard the rasp of a lighter and a deep inhalation of gratitude as he settled in with a cigarette. He was an almost religious smoker who never took the sacrament lightly, treating each white stick reverently, the way the ancient Greeks sang hymns to the gods for their gift of wine that made earthly existence slightly more bearable. I've watched others smoke in some kind of bad trance, hand disconnected from body and mind, robotically lifting the burning stuffed paper to their lips in a rhythm of resigned necessity. Leonard acknowledged each inhalation as a luxury, with a slight smile of wonder at the relaxing, mind-focusing effect of nicotine.

For a brief time I took up smoking if only to share the pleasure with him, consuming a modest daily allotment of fat oval Turkish cigarettes, a much milder strain than Virginia nicotine, according to Leonard's learned recommendation.

But the iconic growl in his voice finally started to thicken into some mess in his throat. His doctor told him he was not merely courting disaster—which would hardly have deterred Leonard, who was courtly in all things—but had already arrived at a dangerous condition. He went cold turkey with nicotine patches.

I asked him what quitting felt like.

"Life seems to have no purpose without smoking."

"What do you know about the Neanderthals?" I began that morning.

"Not much. Just those dim-witted manikins in the natural history museum."

"They got a bad rap. Neanderthals actually had larger brains than we do. But from the archeological evidence, they never changed their tools and fire-making stuff over hundreds of thousands of years. They weren't much into improvement."

"Very sensible people." *Sensible* was one of Leonard's highest compliments. "No wonder we make fun of them."

Warming to my subject, I explained how these gentle souls wandered out of Africa some six hundred thousand years ago, leaving behind their evolutionary-challenged cousins, *us,* smaller, scrawny upright stragglers barely able to eke out an existence on the African plains. Meanwhile the Neanderthals spread out all over Europe and Asia, living contentedly in small groups, not venturing far from their settlements. Then, about sixty thousand years ago, Homo sapiens, long forgotten by the Neanderthals, came charging out of the ancestral homeland, and in practically no time the Neanderthals were gone.

"What happened to them?" Leonard asked like a diligent participant in a campfire tale.

"The better question is: *What happened to us?*"

"We evolved?"

We conducted these joint inquiries with a certain formality, offering rhetorical questions and leaving dramatic pauses as if we were onstage in some empty theater.

"That is the conventional wisdom."

"However, Old Eric has uncovered the dirty little secret they've tried to keep from us. I knew I could count on you!"

I described the oldest prehistoric cave paintings yet discovered—I'd seen them in Werner Herzog's incredible documentary film *Cave of Forgotten Dreams*—wondrous, sophisticated murals depicting fantastic beasts, human hunters and supernatural creatures hovering around them.

"Thirty-two thousand years ago," I emphasized. "Probably in the same caves where Neanderthals lived so long without interior decoration until we wiped them out."

"Was it the triumph of art?"

"Not quite. Neanderthals didn't know what we think we know."

"Elegantly put. But what precisely does it mean?"

"What happened back in Africa? What happened to pathetic little Homo sapiens?"

"Human consciousness!" He practically snapped his fingers.

"Exactly! Some bizarre cross-wiring in our brain that produces the neural static we hear as the disembodied voice-over explaining what the fuck is going on, and we believe every word, because unless we're enlightened or insane, who else can that voice in our heads be except our trusty old self?"

"I hope you're writing all this down."

"Wait. It gets better."

"I'm on the edge of my seat."

"This human *I-consciousness* didn't evolve over millions of years. It happened suddenly."

"A light went on?"

"Something like that."

Each of us possessed different stores of esoteric information gleaned from experience, research, disorganized studies, and our own fertile imaginations. Even though I'm not very good at science per se, I'm inspired by complex theories like relativity, quantum mechanics, and most interesting of all to me—natural selection. A hero of my ex-wife Susan's was Charles Darwin. She, a real scientist, would listen to my improvisational interpretations with remarkable patience, and I took her lack of correction for confirmation, a mistaken assumption on my part that extended far beyond evolution. She had many books about Darwin and the various interpretations of his ideas. I seized upon the catchiest title, *Wonderful Life: The Burgess Shale and the Nature of History*. Its author, Stephen Jay Gould, rejects the classic notion of natural selection as a slow, stately process in which environmental pressures gradually force the adaptations of species. He posits evolution as a series of sudden random mutations that produce a large number of evolutionary losers who quickly disappear—three-eyed shrimp—and a few unpredictable winners. Like us.

"Human consciousness is a random mutation?" Leonard quickly grasped the gist.

"Yup. Could as easily never have happened."

"And it occurred all of a sudden? Not that long ago?"

"Practically yesterday."

"Pretty much the way it's described in Genesis?" He'd grabbed the ball and was racing down the field. "Think about it in biblical time." He paused to let me catch up. "We're in year five thousand seven hundred and seventy-three. There was a long oral tradition around the camp-fire before that, recounting the story of creation that took place *in six days.* That was the creation of I-consciousness, the real story of the Fall from the Garden of Eden, where your beautiful Neanderthals dwelt. And that"—he paused for effect—"is pretty much the way Rebbe Sabbatai Zevi describes it."

Leonard was quite proud: the Jews had it right all along.

By our own self-declarations, Leonard was a Jew and I was not, though he cautioned: *I'm afraid, Old Eric, they won't honor your disclaimer the next time they come to round us up.* Tribal paranoia was a cornerstone of his Jewishness, which was so different from the slack, suburban, humanistic, barely-a-religion practiced by my family in the almost epis-copal atmosphere of the mid-twentieth-century Reformed temple in Westchester, New York, we frequented twice a year on the so-called High Holy Days. God was rarely ref-erenced, certainly not as often as the burning social issues of the day. We were the Chosen People because we sup-ported civil rights for Negroes.

Leonard came from an entirely different milieu. Lofty were the heights of his Westmount neighborhood in Montreal, and he was the scion of one of its most prominent families. His grandfather was a founder of the city's toniest synagogue, his father and uncles princes of the merchant class and proud members of the Commonwealth. As a youth he pressed his ear to the radio, filling his head with images of Hitler's Holocaust, developing a sense of imminent apocalypse he relished his whole life. By contrast, in my youthful world Judgment Day was the fifteenth of April, when acceptance letters from Ivy League colleges arrived in the mail.

Leonard's History of the World was very different from mine. To him 1492 was not the year Columbus's three little ships set sail to discover America, but the date the Jews were expelled from Spain. On his maps countries were shaded in gradient tones from white to pink to bloody red based on the number of Jews killed there in various eras. His tribal membership was a source of comfort to him, but then, he had a general enthusiasm for the rituals and privileges of membership in general.

"I was an avid member of the Canadian Boy Scouts you know. I still have my Scout knife." American Express was his credit card. He got me to join the Executive Health Club at the Hollywood YMCA where he belonged. He observed the Sabbath with candles and a prayer, and after years of tireless effort, he managed to gather both his children, and then his grandchildren, upstairs at Tremaine for Sabbath dinners.

If I was in town on a Friday we'd go shopping together at the Kosher Store—I'm not sure if that's the real name— down on Pico Boulevard and La Brea, wheeling a market basket through the crowded aisles, greeting the family who ran the place, grabbing the perennial staples of his refrigerator: Claussen pickles, sliced Kraft Swiss cheese, sauerkraut, white bread, a broiler chicken, eggs, smoked meat, some fruit, and an occasional vegetable, all somehow kosher. It was comfort food and he wanted to share the comforts with me.

Some thirty years before, on March 11, 1983, a gang wearing long, dark coats invaded our downstairs apartment, faces obscured by thick black beards, heads covered by menacing skullcaps. They stopped and kissed their fingertips with expectant saliva and touched the garish brass mezuzah Leonard had nailed to the doorpost earlier that morning, purchased at a Judaic shop in the nearby Pico-Fairfax community of Orthodox Jews. Leonard warmly welcomed the invaders. The four of them crowded into the tiny hallway, eyes darting around like exterminators looking for signs of termite infestation.

"Where is the mother?" demanded the leader, a hefty rabbi in his fifties.

I pointed mutely to the front room adjoining the kitchen where Susan stood warily, her long fingers wrapped
tightly around the swaddled body of our newborn son,
Samuel Martin Lerner, named for his two Jewish grand-
fathers on my side. The gang approved of that with murmured tribal phrases, some of which I even recognized.

The sight of Susan, though she's only a bit over five
feet tall, seemed to intimidate the rabbi and his minions.
They averted their eyes from Susan's thick mane of brown-
blond hair that hung practically to her waist. Immodesty?
Who can penetrate the minds of the pious?

Leonard, ever the master of manners even in awkward
situations, gently urged the rabbi and his men forward,
whispering to Susan: *It's all right, darling.*

Don't misunderstand Leonard's use of *darling,* a term
of respectful affection with which he addressed a wide
range of females, including his daughter, and later my
daughter, and later his granddaughter, and his girlfriends,
though with them it was less a term of respect than quiet
exasperation. With Susan it was a genuine endearment.
Leonard was quite fond of her and she of him, a mutual
affection that began at our wedding four years earlier at
the Zen Center. Roshi performed the ceremony in the
zendo as Susan and I knelt before him in our black robes.
The party took place in the large adjacent courtyard.
Leonard brought several cases of very good wine. While
I was buzzed on Bordeaux and dancing with all sorts of

friends, Leonard and Susan were engaged in some wonderful dialogue, her strong hands forming animated con-
structions in the air to punctuate her ironic humor for his
amusement.

She was so different from any female he'd ever known,
which was her attraction for me as well from the moment
I met her. She was straightforward and certain in her pronouncements about the way things should and shouldn't
be done, more entertaining than judgmental. She had the
lean, muscular body of the middle-distance runner she'd
been in high school, a body that anchored the slightly
off-kilter mind lurking behind those mismatched eyes,
the earthly brown one a signifier of her practical, compe-
tent side that always kept the kitchen pantry—she called
it the *cupboard*—perfectly stocked and ordered, a marvel
to my sister, while her other eye, an otherworldly green,
or gray, or slightly blue, I could never say for sure, was a
tiny window into an uncharted world of complicated webs.
She was disinclined to flirtation, though guys flirted with
her and I think she enjoyed it. Leonard considered Susan
a brilliant choice on my part—as if there's any choice in
these matters.

~

"You want some young intern practicing his surgical skills
on your son's penis?" Leonard had asked the week before,
handing me a cup of coffee I greatly needed the morning
after my first sleepless night of fatherhood.

We were supposed to call the Santa Monica hospital to make arrangements for Sam's circumcision, but Leonard touted the virtues of a moile, an Orthodox Jewish circumcision specialist, not simply from a medical perspective but an aesthetic one. "These guys are artists," he declared with great conviction.

I didn't much care, but I knew my parents would love a real bris. Leonard volunteered to make the arrangements, except Susan wasn't Jewish, which strictly speaking made our son a goy.

"I know it's asking a lot," Leonard sighed after informing us of the terms of the deal he'd negotiated. The rabbi and his gang would do the bris if Susan agreed to begin a course of guided study after the ceremony and convert to the Jewish faith, making Sam a Jew ex post facto. Susan didn't think it was such a big deal. She was a lapsed Catholic and had already followed me first into Buddhism and then into Roshi's scene. She thought becoming a Jew would be a step up.

At crunch time, though, she seemed to waver. Perhaps it was the sight of the moile, a pale, nervous-looking young zealot, muttering to himself as he opened a beat-up leather attaché case containing his collection of surgical knives, before unfolding a barbaric medieval wooden board on which our son would be strapped down for the procedure. Susan was about to bolt, but Leonard gently took Samuel from her arms, murmuring, "You're supposed to leave the room, darling. By custom."

Handing him over, she announced a bit too loudly, "You think I'd stay and watch?"

My father proudly joined us with his tallis around his shoulders as Leonard and I held up Samuel, strapped to the board. I joined in on the Baruch part of the incantations. The moile pulled down the diaper and, like a samurai wielding his sword, swiped off the debatably expendable portion of flesh.

Then we gathered in our tiny backyard with the traditional bris spread of lox and bagels from Canter's on Fairfax. We'd invited a dozen odd friends, some old spiritual associates and some new business associates. I'd just begun my career in Hollywood.

Who knows, maybe it would have turned out differently if Susan had studied with the Orthodox and converted and we'd become Jews like them? Doubtful. The closest she got was joining the Jewish Community Center on Pico Boulevard so she and Sam could take mommy-and-baby swim classes.

"Quite sensible," was Leonard's final evaluation.

∽

"Want a Popsicle? I laid in a fresh supply before you arrived."

I was visiting him in Los Angeles in May 2013 to continue our discussion of the Neanderthals and the Jews.

We'd spent the early morning in front of the house on the tiny sloping lawn, lounging in his comical outdoor furniture—rickety old paint-peeled, wooden Adirondack chairs. The transformation of the neighborhood since we'd bought Tremaine thirty-five years before was striking. Back then white people of means rarely ventured east of La Cienega Boulevard or south of Olympic, the imaginary Maginot Line of the city after the Watts riots of the sixties. By the turn of the century, though, hipster pioneers had gentrified Echo Park and Silver Lake and the downtown lofts, and now multihued middle-class families populated even our vaguely named Wilshire District, removing the security bars from the windows.

At the beginning Tremaine was pretty much the Lerners' home, a wonderful and curious home with Leonard peripatetically residing upstairs, arriving and departing unexpectedly in those years when his children lived with their mother first in France and then New York City. His career was sustained mostly in Europe and Canada, and returning to Tremaine was a respite from the chaos of his life, the place where he could collapse on his couch in the living room and: *Just rest for a minute or two.*

He kept most of his belongings there, closets and dressers full of clothes and one room crammed with musical instruments and gear. The kitchen cabinets overflowed with stuff from his mother's house in Montreal.

He was always appreciative of the improvements Susan and I made. We ripped up and retiled the kitchen floor downstairs and replaced the crappy stove with a gorgeous old chrome-and-enamel O'Keefe and Merritt that we lugged home from a secondhand store. We transformed the back porch off the bedroom into my writing office.

Sam was quick and mobile at a very early age, and one day at eighteen months old he walked out the front door. I barely caught up with him at the corner as he contemplated crossing six lanes of speeding traffic on Olympic Boulevard. That's when we enclosed the backyard with a chain-link fence, creating Sam's playpen, a little private outdoor space for all of us that would go through many alterations over the decades.

Susan was a constant gardener, a botanical experimentalist exploring new Southern California possibilities. In our folklore of Tremaine her most famous planting was the cedar tree. It was only a four-foot bush when it went into the ground in the small triangular bed near the front door, but it grew like Jack's beanstalk in slow motion, climbing up to Leonard's front door, growing taller and taller until it crept past the roof.

"We finally had to dig out Susan's little tree with a backhoe before the roots tipped the whole house over," Leonard reported somewhat nostalgically around the turn of the century. By then the Lerners' home had become the Cohen family home.

After Susan, Sam, and I moved to Malibu in 1986, we rented the downstairs apartment to a stranger, and Tremaine might have passed out of all our lives if Leonard's daughter, Lorca, hadn't moved in. She was still in high school and Leonard thought she'd be best off living with him. It was only temporary, they both agreed, but a few years later she opened an antique store on Melrose Avenue that would morph into a unique gallery of fantastic objects. She refurbished the O'Keefe and Merritt stove in the downstairs kitchen. Sam's old room became Lorca's daughter's room, and later her infant son slept in my porch-turned-office. Lorca lived at Tremaine for twenty-five years.

Around the same time the cedar tree was uprooted, Leonard finally settled in, furnishing and repairing and repainting and rewiring and air-conditioning Tremaine into an immensely comfortable and comforting place to live. Then his son, Adam, moved down the block with his wife and his son, and somewhat to the amazement of everyone, Leonard had both his children and all his grandchildren surrounding him.

Over the years I would live at several addresses, but Tremaine was always the place that felt most like home whenever I returned. It was the locus of our friendship until the very end.

～

That week I was visiting, the Santa Ana winds were strangely blowing—they usually whip out of the desert in September, not May—driving the temperature up into the nineties by late morning, creating an apocalyptic atmosphere Leonard particularly relished. By midmorning, though, it was too hot even for him, so we went inside. He removed his deconstructed formal attire: old black khaki pants, a threadbare cotton sport jacket of indeterminate gray, and a similarly ancient short-sleeve shirt and skinny tie. Now he was in his house clothes: underwear, a T-shirt, and bare feet. We took our seats in the front room in the two Aeron-type chairs facing the huge Mac monitor on his long antique pine worktable. The room was filled with curios, memorabilia, old photos, various notebooks, writing tools, and quasi-religious symbols of his own creation in various media. Above a small mirror there was a peg rack full of hats.

Even with all this stuff, his workroom was perfectly ordered, almost compulsively, though I hesitate to characterize anything about him as compulsive. Call it an extreme fondness for neatness. For a long time I tried to be a good guest and clean up in the kitchen after a meal or one of our endless snacks. I finally bowed to his insistence that I return to my place at the table beside the window while he wielded sponge and dishrag and paper towels. It was a source of serene pleasure for him to transform small messes into cleanly order, filling the wooden dish rack beside the sink with plates and knives and cups he carefully washed and rinsed, wiping the countertop with a placid, unhurried motion.

That's why he loved hotel rooms. They are so easy to keep tidy with only one door with multiple locks and that most marvelous sign to hang outside: *Do not disturb,* unless you're like me, who can transform a hotel room into chaos minutes after opening my suitcase, clothes strewn over chairs, the bureau cluttered with the detritus of my pockets, unable even to find my toothbrush in the bathroom.

There are aspects of people you're very close to that are so different from yourself they can drive you nuts at times. And then there are other things about them you envy precisely because they are so different from who you are that you imagine your life might be easier if you were more like them. There were certain things Leonard and I envied about each other, though we rarely commented on each other's quirks, and then only matter-of-factly and always with a note of applause.

Leonard and I didn't care much for the advice of others. There were occasions when maybe we should have warned each other: *For God's sakes, man, don't do it!* We rarely did. If one of us forgot ourselves and blurted out a suggestion, a long pause ensued before the offender took it back and repeated our maxim: *Talk is cheap.*

The most we might ever ask was: *So what are you going to do, man?*

Our reply rarely varied—the only appropriate response to intractable circumstances: *I haven't a clue.*

On the rare occasion one of us actually had a plan, like the Charge of the Light Brigade we'd quickly endorse it with the ultimate feckless rallying cry: *It's worth a try!*

Our friendship was a bond of affirmation. We tried to make ourselves clear to each other, clearer than we did to anyone else. We shared a subversive feeling about human life that we hid beneath our shirts like chain mail, burnished with a giddy good humor we did our best to maintain even after we'd been captured and became cellmates, imprisoned for the same careless crimes. To while away our indefinite sentences we concocted an imaginary jigsaw puzzle, perusing the clusters and corners and partially completed borders, pondering the empty spaces that stubbornly resisted our efforts. We'd acquired the puzzle from a mysterious dealer of high-class enigmas in a shop tucked away under a drizzly, dark footbridge over a murky river. The puzzle came in a plain white box, but it wasn't one of those all-white, pictureless puzzles. It was up to us to get the picture. We puzzled over it for forty years, hoping that one day before we were dead we could step back and the whole picture would be clear at last, and like God who made the world in six days, we, too, could take one fucking day off from our exhausting, consuming labors. That was our mad hope, the only one we ever held. If we ever solved the puzzle, it might make things a little easier.

He'd been dying to reveal it to me since I stepped out of the cab the previous morning. He'd almost spilled the beans, unable to resist a teaser. "It's the definitive answer to the Neanderthal question."

Fortified by fresh Popsicles, we settled in before the giant Mac monitor. He was quite adept at digital technology, even though he liked to disguise his aptitude behind a pose of shambling befuddlement, donning a pair of huge old-fashioned reading glasses with thick black frames, his nose practically pressed to the screen. In reality he was always years ahead of me technologically, constantly upgrading his hardware, experimenting early on with voice recognition and drawing programs.

"Let's see now." He clicked and delved. "Here it is."

He leaned back and smiled, curving his small, catlike frame into the chair, relishing his Popsicle. I was struck by how he'd shrunk with age. He really was an Old Boy, though there was no diminishment of his vitality. If anything he had more energy than ever. In his underwear and T-shirt he resembled a wizened elf, light as air, moving almost on tiptoe. Time had treated him so far with tenderness, his hair still thick, his eyes still limpid, creases of experience adding to his quiet authority.

Leonard pointed excitedly to the website he'd loaded. I leaned forward to check out the funky, homemade-looking quasi-Hebraic font.

Leonard read aloud in a sonorous voice:

"The other Jews call me a heretic. Well, I am. And worse, an iconoclast too: my goal is nothing less than the breaking of all religious containers (and not just Judaism) for the sake of liberating God. In the words of my 18th century namesake and predecessor, Yakov Leib Frank, 'All the faiths and conducts and the books that

have been written till today—everyone who reads in them is like
someone who has turned his head backwards and is looking at
things already dead. . . . I worship God *and not religion; I seek*
for His *salvation and not my own . . . or, even less-so, yours. "*

It was signed *Reb Yakov Leib HaKohain.*

Leonard explained that Reb Yakov Leib HaKohain,
born Lawrence G. Corey, presented himself as fully enlightened in the lineage of Sri Ramakrishna, as well as the
true heir and modern interpreter of Sabbatai Zevi, the
"Jewish Avatar," a seventeenth-century Sephardic rabbi
who claimed to be the Messiah. Sabbatai Zevi founded a
mystic sect in Constantinople and later converted to Islam
to avoid execution, though it is unclear if he was in greater
danger from the sultan or his fellow Jews for his subversive
Kabbalistic teachings.

Leonard was a dues-paying member of the community
of Donmeh West, founded by Reb Yakov Leib HaKohain,
which numbered about a thousand.

"He's brilliant. Totally mad of course," Leonard offered by way of recommendation. The rebbe conveyed
his teachings via video lectures and podcasts, the juici-
est of which Leonard had cued up for me. Over the next
two days, fueled by our stash of Popsicles, analgesics, and
sundry snacks, I studied with Leonard as countless gener-
ations of Talmudists before us had studied. After all, he
reminded me with a look of mock pride, he was a *Kohain*
from the ancient priestly tribe.

Leonard spun his exegesis in a language entirely his own. He never really updated his vocabulary with the times, eschewing the passing hip for the perennial cool. He mixed the terminology of circa 1953 Beats with phrases of Anglo-Canadian upper-class usage the way some black guys effortlessly mix proper English with jive in a single paragraph, even in a single sentence: *impeccable, like a million bucks, haughty, bro, top-notch, a stand-up guy, out of sight.* His hand solemnly slicing the air for emphasis, he deciphered the indecipherable for me.

Leonard could have been a great rabbi, but he was a poet, not a teacher. The difference was clear to both of us. A teacher seeks to be embraced for his teachings, presenting himself as a channel, if not the actual embodiment of the truth of what he teaches, be it the essence of Buddhism or the themes in Thomas Hardy's fiction. The poet, on the other hand, creates a persona, a ventriloquist's dummy whose utterances deflect any further inquiry into his own heart and mind.

Leonard was a master of persona.

~

Reb Yakov Leib HaKohain intoned:

A fundamental and revolutionary teaching of early Sabbatianism . . . was that the God of Creation and the God of Israel were "different" Gods—or at least different emanations of God—and that while the God of Creation was central to nominal Judaism, it was the God of Israel (or, as Frank would later call Him, "Big Brother") that was the God of the Faith of Sabbatai Zevi.

Leonard hit the pause button. "That's the basic point. There were two Creations and there are two Gods."

"One real God and one imaginary God?" I ventured.

"Exactly!" He was pleased I was getting it so quickly. Now we could be persecuted together, like Sabbatai Zevi back in old Constantinople.

"A good God and a bad God. For our purposes." In the first creation, Leonard explained, the Real Creation, God, the Good God, the God of the Faith, manifested not as the One God the Jews are so proud of having invented, but rather God as One.

(Don't strain yourself trying to comprehend. Simply savor the flavor.)

"But then"—Leonard unfolded himself from his chair, leaning forward, elbows on knees, voice low and secretive—"humans came along and we made up our own version of what happened. That's the Second Creation: how in one week God was created and then He created us in his own image. But in fact . . ." He paused, letting me catch up with the story. "As Sabbatai Zevi explains, we created this God in *our* image. He's a total figment of our imagination. He's as fucked up as we are, or worse: a jealous, judgmental, anxiety-ridden, psychopathic killer. We feel better about Him that way. That's why Reb Yakov Leib HaKohain declares his mission is to 'repair' the 'Face of God'!"

"That's terrific!"

"It ain't bad."

"It's fantastic!" I insisted

"It's all just spiritual porn. At least this is a high-class variety. Another Popsicle?"

After we'd sucked our fresh Popsicles clean to the stick, I observed that in the first creation, the Real Creation, the Good God and the Neanderthals arose as One. That was the true Garden of Eden, filled with creatures who lacked any awareness of their Limited Self.

"I don't know about you," he went on, rhetorically, because of course he knew about me. "I always feel like I'm not getting it quite right. The Neanderthals didn't give a shit. If they had a little hammer and it worked, they used it for a hundred thousand years."

"And they didn't need to paint crazy stories about themselves on their cave walls."

We took this idea and riffed on it for a while. We often riffed, improvising off the melody. We'd start out playing it straight, like Coltrane did with "My Favorite Things," where you can practically sing along with him as he plays the melody the first time. *Raindrops on roses* . . . Then he plays it a second time, dropping some of the accents, short-handing the phrases, and then he abandons the melody entirely and riffs, following the chords, creating original, improvisatory revelations, the way Leonard was riffing on the Neanderthals, painting his own improbable, captivating diorama. Unlike the dusty cavemen behind the thick glass in natural history museums, Leonard's natural men and women stood *outside* the glass, curiously examining the tortured Homo sapiens imprisoned within their own imaginations, wrestling with their guilt and their angst and their fear of God's wrath.

"No wonder our ancestors wiped them out," Leonard finally concluded.

"But they didn't entirely." It was my turn for a startling revelation. By adding *Neanderthals* to my Google News alerts, I'd learned of a new study by some guys who sequenced the DNA from actual Neanderthal bones and compared it to the human genome. They concluded that, on average, individual living Europeans and Asians have between 1 and 4 percent Neanderthal in their DNA.

"So we fucked the women and killed the guys," Leonard observed. "Neanderthal pogroms."

"Think about this, though. If one to four percent Neanderthal DNA is an *average* in humans today, then some people have no Neanderthal in them, and other people have more than four percent."

"Very interesting."

"I like to think I have a bit more myself." I could confide these things to him.

"I'm sure you do."

"Makes you wonder."

"It does."

We wondered. We pondered. We looked at each other.

"Roshi could be a hundred percent Neanderthal?" I finally ventured.

"Or pretty close."

Did we have the missing piece at last? Could we finally fill the gaping hole in our puzzle and answer the most pressing question of our lives, or at least one of them?

What the fuck is Roshi all about?

three

ZERO

ALMOST THIRTY-FIVE YEARS EARLIER in the fall of 1979, a few months after we bought Tremaine at a probate auction, Leonard waited for me in his black Zen robes at the top of our small front lawn that sloped steeply to the street, a thick mat of savage growth diligently crew-cut by the old Japanese gardener, Jack, whom we inherited with the house. Jack showed up once a week wearing a heavy khaki uniform complete with pith helmet, running a massive gang-mower over our tiny patch of grass. He spoke about as much English as Roshi did, indecipherable over the roar of his backpack blower with which he completed his tonsorial efforts. He mostly ignored us, as if the house was as much his as ours.

I emerged into the predawn darkness that morning and quietly pulled the new metal-mesh security door closed behind me and locked it, not quite sure what to do with the key since my robes had no pockets. I dropped it into the sleeve.

Leonard practically skipped down to his little faded green Volkswagen parked at the curb, a mini-wagon they long ago stopped selling in the States, a curiously downscale vehicle for a pop star to drive in LA. Beneath the streetlights our shins and bare feet in flip-flops looked ghostly white.

"Let's get out of here," he whispered dramatically. "Before they shoot us." The vague, apocalyptic *they*. "For many reasons."

We buckled up like two bomber pilots heading into the wild blue yonder, nothing but our underwear beneath our black dresses at this chilly hour on the edge of the ghetto. We drove down to Pico and then picked up San Vicente, angling east and farther south onto the Santa Monica Freeway.

We'd done a daylight test run before we bought the house but this was our first real mission. Leonard had phoned me the night before with the red alert that Roshi was in town and giving sanzen that morning. As Leonard drove he checked his worn Swiss army watch with the face on the inside of his wrist, keeping me posted on our running time.

"Seven minutes."

We swung off the freeway at Arlington, an exit no reasonable white person took except the determined few whose destination was Cimarron Zen Center.

"Eleven minutes!" His excitement was rising. "This is terrific!"

Leonard's respect for playing hooky was informed by his equally serious respect for the demands of duty, responsibility, and work. He understood that you can't enjoy the exquisite pleasure of getting off the hook—*hooky!*—if you haven't put in your time dangling from it.

While I was no longer cloaking my spiritual practice in the puffy down of selfless nobility worn so proudly by New Age enthusiasts then and now who claim that their efforts somehow elevate the consciousness of the entire world, I still pursued it intently as a utilitarian activity, part of my work. But Leonard would always see it as getting away with something, slipping the traces and galloping off on a morning like this to play riddles with a fat little Japanese guy instead of pressing our noses to the grindstone.

In high spirits he glanced in the rearview mirror and declared, "They'll never catch us!"

In the darkness the elegant old Craftsman-style houses of the once upscale West Adams neighborhood flew by. We passed Roshi's house with its wide pillared porch and the two houses that served as residences for the students and monks who lived at the Zen Center, as I had with Susan for a year before we bought Tremaine.

Leonard swung around the corner on Cimarron Street and we almost hit a pickup truck parked in the short drive-way beside the door in the high stucco wall embedded with shards of glass, not to keep the acolytes in but to keep the local gangbangers out of the urban American Zen temple.

"Thirteen minutes!" he whispered as we walked past the dining hall and up the steps to the zendo with the clap-pers still sounding. We kicked off our flip-flops alongside twenty other pairs of assorted footgear, and then gathered ourselves for a deep bow upon entering. Palms held to-gether we walked beside the raised platform of black mats and cushions until we found two empty spots. The clappers ceased as we tucked ourselves into place and breathed in the intoxicating aroma of lightly perfumed incense, resid-ual spiritual sweat, and a whiff of night-blooming jasmine from the courtyard outside, like the scent of a woman that dizzies you and obliterates rational thought. As the final bell commenced zazen, Leonard shot me a glance, raising both eyebrows: *How great is this?*

He always enjoyed rituals more than I did, not out of any sense of belief, but for the simple pleasure of perform-ing them.

There was nothing grand or elegant about the zendo, although the high ceiling was nice. It bore little resem-blance to a high-class Japanese temple built of rare wood

and fine metalwork. It was knocked together out of functional materials like plywood, built by students possessing
various degrees of construction skill. There was no particular message or spiritual teaching in this modesty of presentation. Roshi wasn't into money or its display. It was
a personal preference, and like his many other preferences—cognac over vodka—people could emulate them
or not. He didn't care. Leonard and I actually liked the
threadbare atmosphere of Roshi's scene.

Leonard wasn't at Mt. Baldy when I arrived at Roshi's
training center in December 1977, a little more than
six months after the Saint Joseph's Abbey sesshin where
Roshi had either suggested, invited, or ordered me to
come study with him.

On the edge of Claremont, one of the nicest small cit-
ies in Southern California with its five colleges and wide,
tree-shaded streets—a lovely place to reside if you were
so inclined as opposed to us, desperate desperadoes zip-
ping through as quickly as possible to the outskirts—you
ran smack into an eight-thousand-foot mountain, like a giant spaceship landed. A narrow road without guardrails
switchbacked up the mountain beside an unstable cliff
side shedding a light shower of sand that without warning
could turn into a storm of falling boulders. It got wilder
still leaving Mount Baldy Village at four thousand feet, an

outpost of outliers, one of those places in the mountains and deserts of Southern California with a post office and a few supply stores, whose residents are determined to maintain their distance from civilization.

I can still recall the feeling driving up the mountain for the first time, the same feeling I had every time Leonard and I drove up over the years in his Nissan Pathfinder, an incongruously macho vehicle he bought for just this purpose, powerful enough to get through the snow drifts that sometimes blocked the road in winter above five thousand feet. We called it: *Getting out of Dodge.*

I arrived that first winter without a return ticket. I was twenty-eight. Everything I owned was packed into an army surplus duffel bag and an unwieldy wooden box of carpenter's tools. After returning from my Buddhist journey to the East in 1974, I'd moved into a communal farm in western Massachusetts where Ivy League graduates like myself entered the building trades and agricultural industry without training or qualification. The uniform alone sufficed: Dunham work boots (predecessor in hip of Timberlands), a wool shirt with grease stains and an ostentatious hole or two, possibly the result of a work-related injury, and a well-worn leather carpenter's tool belt. But I was also a writer! An *author* even, with a picture of myself on the dust jacket of my book sporting a beatific smile in my Pendleton shirt.

～

"Hai. Koan," Roshi demands.

"How do I realize my true nature looking at the pine tree?"

Roshi's eyes fly open as if shaken awake.

"Elic."

Unbelievable. He remembers my name. Did he know I was coming to Baldy following his command? Or is this a wonderful surprise for him?

He rings his little bell, dismissing me with a smirk.

Later that morning I step out of a chemical toilet into a Japanese landscape painting, a tiny solitary figure in a stunning vista of snow clinging to facades of huge conifers, one of which could be the pine tree Roshi wants me to look at and realize my true nature.

"Hai. Koan."

"How do I realize my true nature looking at the pine tree?"

"How DO you realize true nature looking at the pine tree?"

What is there to say? I know other students say things to Roshi, sometimes engaging him in repartee whose exact words I can't make out from the sanzen waiting room as I sit in the next-student-up chair, holding a mallet poised in the air beside a beautiful bronze bell hanging on a wooden stand, concentrating on not only answering my koan but hearing the tinkle of Roshi's bell dismissing the student in front of me, the signal for me to smack my big bell in response, indicating, as I've been instructed: *I hear you loud and clear, Roshi, and I'm coming!*

The student before me holds the door open and stands aside so she won't get knocked over as I charge by and fling myself down in the prescribed bows and prostrations. I'm breathless. But I'm *still.* At least I'm trying to be still. It feels more like I'm holding a handful of water in two cupped hands, trying not to spill my answer before I demonstrate how I realize my true nature looking at the pine tree.

My eyes widen and my head tilts back. My face is a mask of wonderment. The pine tree looms large in my mind. I shut my eyes tight, the way Miles Davis used to play his solos in front of an audience so he wouldn't get distracted. In the dark I wait for Roshi to say something, hopefully approving.

"Too much thinking," he casually remarks.

I reluctantly bow to his tinkling dismissal bell, muttering in my mind: *I was not thinking well maybe I was but I won't next time.* I narrowly avoid the next charging student at the door.

∽

"Hai. Koan."

"How do I realize my true nature . . ." A pause, a confident pause, 'cause I've got this sucker by the neck. ". . . when I am looking at the pine tree?"

I rise up on my knees. I even stand up as the awed awesomeness of my true nature fills the room, threatening to explode the walls, the pine tree growing to a hundred feet tall. *Ta-daaaaa.* Check this shit *out,* Roshi.

Roshi briefly considers my performance. "Sixty percent."

What?

He stares at me until I get it: he's *grading* my performance. I'm not sure if 60 percent is an F for Failing or if he's calculated that Elic has realized 60 percent of his true nature and missed the other 40 percent, in which case I'm encouraged rather than crushed. Hey, 60 percent in this game sounds good to me.

"Roshi reminds me of my freshman football coach, Big Dan Woodard," I once told Leonard.

"What a great name."

"A great man. I loved him dearly. He had this suave mustache and aged, coffee-color skin. He was once a linebacker for the Cleveland Browns, before he became a social studies teacher and coach. He had a crooked leg below a shattered knee that ended his pro football career and led him to his true calling: instructor in the fine art of blocking and tackling. He was a master. And no martinet. Big Dan got right in there with us, wearing his sweats: *There you go, baby, use the forearm shiver! The way I showed you! Like this, like this! Get your leverage, stay low, drive, drive, drive. Better. Yeah, better.* What a ton of fun he was to play with. Like Roshi. Know what I mean?"

"Metaphorically speaking."

Mmm. Maybe seventy percent.

More. More. Whole body. Whole cosmos.

Tsk. Better last time.

Like Big Dan, Roshi gives instruction in the fine points of the technique of manifesting true self.

~

As I previously noted, the encounter between student and Roshi in the sanzen room is supposed to have the sanctity of the Catholic confessional. Eventually, though, Leonard and I transgressed and revealed to each other—*I'll show you mine if you show me yours*—how our sanzens went. It turned out that we "answered" our koans in very different ways. I answered with my body. I think I answer everything with my body. Leonard sometimes wished he could answer more things with his body. On the other hand, I was awed by Leonard's gift for the compression of words.

~

Roshi says nothing. No *Hai, koan.* No *Hai, Elic.* Silence.

I forge ahead. "How do I realize my true nature looking at the pine tree?"

He's waiting.

Then I realize my true nature looking at the pine tree, manifesting absolute self with my whole body, or at least enough to satisfy him for the moment.

He grunts in affirmation.

I'm very excited. Now what? Am I enlightened? Am I the next Roshi? Does my shit no longer stink?

"Hai. Koan."

I'm confused. Does Roshi want me to do it again?

Not quite.

"How do you realize your true nature looking at ants crawling on the ground?"

Another koan. Ants this time. A bit of a surprise.

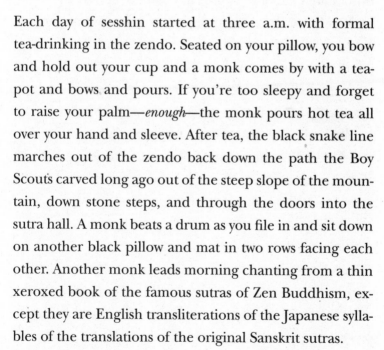

Each day of sesshin started at three a.m. with formal tea-drinking in the zendo. Seated on your pillow, you bow and hold out your cup and a monk comes by with a tea-pot and bows and pours. If you're too sleepy and forget to raise your palm—*enough*—the monk pours hot tea all over your hand and sleeve. After tea, the black snake line marches out of the zendo back down the path the Boy Scouts carved long ago out of the steep slope of the mountain, down stone steps, and through the doors into the sutra hall. A monk beats a drum as you file in and sit down on another black pillow and mat in two rows facing each other. Another monk leads morning chanting from a thin xeroxed book of the famous sutras of Zen Buddhism, except they are English transliterations of the Japanese syllables of the translations of the original Sanskrit sutras.

Huh?

HO-HA-HE-HU-DO-TA-RE-RI.

Ten pages of this is purportedly the Heart Sutra.

It's verbal jumping jacks in the snow to get the blood flowing, certainly not to enlighten you with the meaning of the Heart Sutra. The syllables mean absolutely nothing, not even to the senior monks who've memorized them, all the better to snooze as the drum beats faster and faster and the chanting becomes cacophony, tickling my funny bone. I recall the celestial voice of Cantor Smolover at the JCC temple of my youth leading the choir and congregation in Shema Yisrael, words to thrill, to elevate, to believe in. We, however, are grunting utter nonsense at goofball speed at three thirty in the morning.

But it works!

We finish chanting and march out in unison back up the long path to the zendo, and not even the most imaginative among us entertains a single thought or consideration regarding the meaning of the Heart Sutra, much less Buddhism, much less Zen. This ignorance is vital to the teaching of Joshu Sasaki Roshi.

Hours later it is still only midmorning. After zendo and more zendo and sanzen and breakfast and more zendo, we march back down to the sutra hall. This time Roshi enters accompanied by the head monk, whom he berates for getting the details of his ceremonial entrance wrong, even though the monk is doing exactly what Roshi told him to do the day before, after Roshi berated him then for getting it wrong. Roshi takes his seat at the head of the room and his translator settles in beside him.

The talk, or sermon, is a fixture of all religions: old, ancient, conventional, radical, Eastern, Western, or New Age. It reiterates and expounds upon the beliefs that encourage, admonish, and inspire the congregation on the path to wherever they hope they're going, reminding them that whoever is not on this path is at best lost in delusion and at worst damned for eternity.

Alas, Roshi's daily talks, his *teisho*, were more reminiscent of morning chanting: incomprehensible transliterations of a translation of some coded linguistic representation of reality.

He really gave only one teisho over and over again. In painstaking, often mind-numbing detail, employing metaphors like the complementary and opposite forces of positive and negative, or the attraction, coming together, and repulsion of man and woman, Roshi related how he experienced the activity of consciousness: *Zero is the center of gravity.*

This is from one of his teisho:

Once you experience this absolute self you will clearly comprehend the repetitious function of life: the individual self dissolving in the realization of absolute self, followed by the breaking up of the absolute, as the individual self arises again to dissolve anew in the absolute. This repetitious function is described as sunyata *or emptiness, I call this the function of zero. The only self that we can actually affirm is this self-activity that is the function of zero.*

Leonard and I agreed that you rarely walked away from his talks with that special sensation most congregants crave from their church or temple, mosque or New Age meditation retreat, the most comforting taste religion has to offer: the pap of smug.

Ha! We're Jews! We invented monotheism! And we have higher SAT scores than you goyim!

Ha! We're Christians and Christ is our Savior and not yours, so we're going to Heaven and you are going straight to HELL!

Ha! We're Buddhists, not even old Buddhists, but new, American, better Buddhists and we practice the Dharma and you don't, so we know what's going on, because we're Mindful and you're Mindless! Ha! Ha! HAH!

After that first winter I studied with him, Roshi said to me: *Buddhism is not a club.* He subverted all beliefs, ideas, consensual morality, and any pose of piety you tried to strike, be it imitative Japanese or the bullshit New Age posture of equanimity. He pried your fingers loose from any rock of comfort you clung to in the treacherous waters of human life and laughed if you drowned. Instead of a beatific smile, Roshi offered a sarcastic smirk.

I didn't realize how much I detested smug until I met Roshi. I was pretty smug getting accepted to Harvard,

World Headquarters of the League of Smug, and smugger still becoming a Buddhist, a much more exclusive affiliation I believed at the time. I was so smug I recommended it for whatever ails you, all of you. I even made my poor parents attend a Vipassana meditation retreat. I was insufferable.

Roshi revivified my latent subversive streak, a sensibility that can barely tolerate conventional wisdom, preferring to turn all expressions of belief upside down or inside out. That had always been Leonard's inclination, too, though you won't find much of it in his early songs. He didn't aspire to the career of Frank Zappa. Read his novel *Beautiful Losers*. Read his fall-down-laughing, mordant manifesto, *Death of a Lady's Man*. Read his poems.

Roshi was virtually unknown outside of his relatively tiny scene when I arrived at Baldy that winter in 1978. He hadn't published anything, while Joseph Goldstein and Jack Kornfield and Chögyam Trungpa and Suzuki Roshi and Ram Dass and Bubba Free John and countless others were churning out volumes of talks and teaching. Some even had their own publishing companies.

But almost no one knew of the brilliance of Joshu Sasaki Roshi.

Or Eric Lerner!

Yeah, there was plenty of that in my latest inspiration: *Eric has once more found the real deal, and here it is!*

After that first winter with Roshi I wanted to go public with my subversive self. I wanted to vanquish the insufferable pietists, no matter how insufferable I might be.

∿

Like mad scientists Leonard and I passed a magnifying loupe back and forth, squinting at the images on a contact sheet of photographs by Ralph Gibson, whose work was shown regularly in his New York City gallery and published in expensive editions. Gibson was an old friend of Leonard's. He'd graciously accepted Leonard's invitation to contribute one of his signature pieces for the cover of the first issue of our new journal, *Zero*. We peered at the images of a strikingly beautiful blond woman shading her eyes from some off-camera light. Though only her head and shoulders are in the frame, there is an unmistakable suggestion that she is entirely naked.

"Hard to choose," Leonard admitted, comparing one pose to another.

"Mmm," I agreed. It was probably the first time we conversed in the tone that became our lingua franca. It bore a superficial resemblance to the humor of junior high school boys, frat bros, and aging movie producers, eternally sophomoric and *South Park*. But what elevated it—at least we liked to think so—was never dissolving into a sniggering crack-up that admitted the joke, never wavering from our deadpan delivery, creating a double irony that made the joke more serious than what was being joked about.

We were just getting to know each other that morning in the fall of 1978 as we examined Ralph Gibson's photos. We were still uncertain about the depth of each other's subversive sensibilities, so it was a pleasant revelation to find ourselves in complete agreement. The beautiful naked blond, framed in a black border, with the vaguely calligraphic logo of *Zero* above the subtitle, *Contemporary Buddhist Life and Thought,* was the perfect cover for the first issue of our new journal!

As a kind of counterpoint, or exclamation point, to the blond on the front cover, we presented this effusive poem of praise that Allen Ginsberg had given us on the back:

Subtle understand of glad emptiness of our lives
American Earthly saves us from Apocalyptic Pain,
The "Suffering of Suffering," so a XXth Century
Literature of Dharma Bums and Ladies & Gentlemen
rises in Capitals & Provinces, exemplified herein Zero.

Ginsberg wasn't part of Roshi's scene. He was a serious student of the Tibetan master Chögyam Trungpa Rinpoche, but his poetry appeared in *Zero,* along with Pulitzer Prize winners John Ashbery and James Tate. We published Gary Snyder and Paul Bowles, lengthy interviews with John Cage, Kenneth Rexroth, and Joni Mitchell, a portfolio by the rock 'n' roll photographer Norman Seeff, who'd just completed a shoot with the Rolling Stones. We did a long piece on the Jamaican rap poet Linton Kwesi Johnson.

The enterprise had Roshi's support in part because Leonard was an advisory editor. He also subsidized the renovation of an old garage behind a Cimarron residential house that we turned into an editorial office complete with desk and phone for the editor.

Leonard promised to "contribute something" to the first issue. He dropped by the office one morning with a sheaf of unpublished proof pages. *Death of a Lady's Man* is a slim volume of poems and prose poems, each followed by an identically titled pseudo-commentary by the author of the poems. It's deadpan hilarious, one of my favorite things he ever created.

He sat smoking cigarettes, handing me one page after another to read at my desk and choose a selection. Leonard was ever the formalist. I was the editor and he the contributor.

Zero was printed in the style of the great literary journals of the day, like the *Paris Review*. Each issue contained color portfolios of art and photography on glossy paper. Leonard always kept them on his shelf at Tremaine to show friends, a much better explanation of what Roshi was about than any verbal exegesis he never wished to make.

We published four issues in all, biannually for two years, and attracted a circulation of three thousand, impressive for a little journal at that time.

The cover of the second issue featured an Arab boy in a djellaba with an upright violin on his knee and a bow in

hand. It was our "music" issue. For our finale, we took a
weird Buddhist statue of a skeleton and made it very, very
Far Eastern by setting it against an electric-yellow background and putting a photo of a slightly mad, shirtless
Miles Davis on the back to complement the skeleton.

We did publish some "rocks and water stuff," new translations of Sino/Japanese/Buddhist classics like Basho and
Gensei, to round out the riddle: What in the world is *Contemporary Buddhist Life and Thought?*

We gave some hints, like a portfolio entitled "Achieve-
ment," a selection of kitschy 1950s photos from the collection of Mal Sharpe, a Hollywood standup comedian and
sketch writer. They were utterly goofy Southern California
images, like a child in a tuxedo proudly blowing a trumpet
and a blindfolded silent-film stuntman throwing knives at
two bikini-clad models.

Get it?

Contemporary Buddhist Life and Thought is a joke.

The last word on the matter was the teisho by Joshu
Sasaki Roshi, which I quoted from earlier. He was in a
good enough mood to let me publish it.

~

Not long after the first issue appeared, we moved into the
house on Tremaine in the summer of 1979. For anyone in
Roshi's scene, there was always another, more mundane
koan to solve: How do you continue studying with him

if you don't become one of his monks? His community around Cimarron Zen Center was a dysfunctional scene, as most spiritual communities were back then and probably will be forever. Leonard never considered living there and I was glad to move out. On the other hand, we didn't want to be mere weekend churchgoers. Tremaine was our brilliant solution, a halfway house, halfway in the world and halfway to Roshi. We could run off in the middle of the night in our black dresses and return as the sun came up to carry on with our endeavors.

They'll never catch us, Old Eric!

We hoped.

～

That morning recounted at the beginning of this chapter, after our maiden voyage to the zendo, we drove back and parked in front of Tremaine. The little old Chinese woman from the house next door came out as her American-born son arrived to drop off her grandson for the day while he went to work. She looked at Leonard and me in our ridiculous outfits and turned away, embarrassed.

"Wanna come up for a cup of coffee?" Leonard offered.

I followed him upstairs. The front room was still filled with cardboard boxes sealed with packing tape. The week before, Leonard had asked me to give him a hand.

"I have to pick up some stuff."

～

He wore one of his best Armani suits as we drove west on San Vicente, then wended our way up Laurel Canyon to Woodrow Wilson Drive.

It was a grand house. Not Beverly Hills grand but perfectly grand, the way *Leonard Cohen* ought to live, at the top of the Hollywood Hills above the booming music business, the record labels and studios and clubs and agents and lawyers down below on Sunset. Even though his most recent album, produced by the legendarily hip Phil Spector, had been a flop commercially and even artistically, it was cool, especially the cover photo of Leonard with an exotically beautiful black-haired woman leaning against him, Suzanne—not *the* Suzanne, he must have corrected a thousand times, but the mother of his kids. They were out on the town and there was another woman half in the frame, on the other side of him. He's got a cigarette in hand, placidly cool, even though Suzanne looks pissed. The album cover is a *cover*, and so is the title, *Death of a Ladies' Man,* similar to the book. It's a multilayered confession of surrender.

∽

The dry cleaning.

That became our shorthand for the story he told me later.

"I was working in my office upstairs, a little room I'd managed to claim for myself. I'm not complaining. That's what I do, I get up every day and work and now I'm a husband and a father, so I've got to work harder. Writing songs wasn't an indulgence. It paid the bills. She walked in and dumped a load of clothes on the floor and asked me if I'd drop them off at the dry cleaners when I went out.

"Did I say I was going out?

"You know what it's like to get a line or two down on paper, Old Eric, to get the concentration going and string a few thoughts together you might sell for a buck or two. And if the thread snaps, your day is shot. You might as well drop off the dry cleaning."

He tried to hold his life together with chewing gum and Scotch tape. Before he sat down to a day's work, punched in at the factory, he'd tiptoe out of the house in the middle of the night and drive across town to sit in the zendo and meet Roshi in sanzen. Sometimes he'd go up to Baldy and sometimes he'd get on a plane with Roshi. He managed to juggle all the plates in the air until they crashed on his head.

～

He hadn't been back to the house up on Woodrow Wilson Drive since it was emptied of furniture, clothes, his kids, and their mother. The dust hadn't been swept clean; it had only just settled. We found the room where the heavy cardboard moving boxes packed with his stuff were piled, and we carried them down a steep flight of hillside steps to his car.

After we packed up the car he locked the door of the house behind him, muttering, "I have to drop these keys somewhere I can't quite recall at the moment." We sat on the patio overlooking the city below, and he smoked a cigarette, giving me an opportunity to take it all in, the big picture. The details would come later.

He was the one who'd decided on our friendship. He'd had other close friends, but at a certain point he couldn't explain his life to anyone, even if he'd had the inclination, which he didn't. He understood, as I would come to understand, that the explanation is always a plea for the defense. Somehow he determined that I could understand him without explanation. It wouldn't have occurred to me to try to establish a friendship with him, the kind I'd had with other like-minded characters over the years, not because he was *Leonard Cohen*, and not even because of the disparity in our ages, but because of his reserve, the wall of manners and formality he'd erected as if to deliberately contradict the exhausting, frenetic openness of that era.

He knew me better than I knew myself back then. I'd only just turned thirty, but he knew I was heading into the same difficult waters he was treading, fighting the riptide and the undertow. He knew I would struggle like him not to go under. How did he know? I was feeling pretty jaunty, full of confidence and bluster, but he knew it was a long shot at best. He was kind enough to keep his estimation to himself for a while.

~

He had a brand-new coffeemaker in the kitchen, his most important appliance, and he fired it up that morning after we got back to Tremaine from the zendo. He dumped the coffee from the can into the filter without measuring and filled the water well to the top.

"Oops." He discovered you couldn't interrupt the cycle to pour a cup. We waited patiently until all twelve cups dripped through. "Ahh," he exhaled approvingly after his first sip. "This is terrific! Our little house!"

It was terrific. After meeting the master we were hanging out in our black robes drinking coffee with no one around to ask him to drop off the dry cleaning. We each had a fulfilling day of work ahead of us, and tomorrow morning we'd make another trip to see the wizard. I held out my cup for a refill.

Then we froze, listening closely to the sound of human movement beneath us. Susan was awake.

Susan who?

Didn't I leave her back in Massachusetts with no promises when I headed for Mt. Baldy without a return ticket?

Oh, right. Roshi married us last April.

After that first winter with Roshi I felt better than I'd ever felt in my entire life. I felt so good I bummed a bunch of quarters from my fellow students of Zen and raced down the path and across the road to Earl's Lodge, not for a burger but to use the pay phone. A few weeks later Susan arrived by cross-country bus, looking delectable, her long hair cascading over her thin blue cotton dress, carrying one suitcase and a guitar. A suitcase and a guitar! Classic.

Now she was downstairs and we were married.

But there was nothing to fear. I could maintain my true purpose in life, or one of them—getting enlightened under the tutelage of Joshu Sasaki Roshi—proof of which were the robes I was wearing, even while I pursued other purposes in my life, proof of which was Susan, my wife, who slept beside me in our bed beside my writer's office. I could do it all.

Just like Leonard!

He smiled benevolently, tragically, and went over to the open window and shouted, "We're up here, darling. Having coffee. Come and join us."

He turned and whispered to me, "You don't want the little creature to think you ran away."

～

Roshi demands: "Hai, koan."

Elic speaks: "How do I explain why Bodhidharma came from the West while I'm hanging from a tree branch by my teeth with a hungry tiger pacing beneath me?"

It took a few sanzens to even understand what Roshi meant, not the "answer" but the question itself.

Bodhidharma, depicted in Japanese brushwork paintings as a scowling, bearded, crazy-eyed barbarian, is revered

as the patriarch who brought the teachings of Zen from India to China, from whence it migrated to Japan. In this
koan, as Roshi repeated several times before I got it: *Why
Bodhidharma came from West is same as true nature, same as
Buddha nature.*

Okay, so I'm hanging from a tree branch, actually more
like a limb, by my teeth, *no hands, no hands,* and there's this
tiger nipping at my bare feet. *Hungry tiger.* And I'm supposed to manifest my true nature. Quite a predicament.

However, unlike looking at a pine tree or watching
ants crawling, or other things I'd been able to do while
realizing true nature, I'd never been in this predicament.
In the sanzen room I was in a fifth-grade play, pretending
to be Abraham Lincoln with black fuzz Scotch-taped to
my chin. Which was my bad, because of course I was very
much in this predicament when Roshi gave me the koan,
only I didn't know it yet.

Roshi sent me packing, gently, with his best wishes.

Elic, you take Zero. *My present. Mmmm. Still student. But
you go now.*

Over the years, Leonard and I discussed and dissected
Roshi's gesture. One interpretation—based on a certain
fantasy about the wisdom of the master—was that Roshi
decided Elic must solve his koan by experiencing the koan
of human life—you know, it's *all* hanging by your teeth
with a hungry tiger nipping at your heels. Another interpretation was that *Zero* really pissed off Roshi's wife. It was

hardly the prestigious scholarly journal she envisioned that would elevate her husband's stature back in Japan and in the halls of American academia. She considered it a profane embarrassment. Roshi did the math and calculated that by getting rid of *Zero* he'd mollify her complaints about his diddling around with various females in the community.

"That's a distinct possibility," Leonard noted.

But Roshi didn't have to give me *Zero*. I published two more issues from a little office on La Brea Boulevard, and everyone knew *Zero* was still him. He didn't have to send me packing with his best wishes. He'd sent plenty of others packing without them, not to mention those he didn't send packing but made so miserable they stormed out cursing him.

He never sent Leonard packing, but Leonard had to go, too. He had mouths to feed. Not long after we moved into Tremaine, our brilliant solution, Leonard hit the road for years, returning periodically to collapse on the couch before departing for various hotel rooms or the trailer in the French countryside beside the farmhouse he bought for Suzanne, to spend time with his young children.

We were still Roshi's students, but for a long time we didn't see him much. We were too busy hanging from the tree branch by our teeth, avoiding the hungry tiger, to consider why Bodhidharma came from the West.

four

MARCH OF THE PENGUINS

AT THE END OF each Antarctic summer, the emperor penguins of the South Pole journey to their traditional breeding grounds in a fascinating mating ritual captured in an amazing documentary by the French filmmaker Luc Jacquet. The journey across frozen tundra proves to be the simplest part of the ritual for the penguins. After the egg is hatched, the female must delicately transfer it to the male and make her way back to the distant sea to nourish herself and bring food back to her newborn chick. As the narrator, Morgan Freeman, gently intones in his tremulous voice-over at the beginning of the film: *It's a love story.*

It was one of our all-time favorite movies. I'm not sure which of us saw it first and recommended it to the other, but we watched it together once on the giant-screen TV in his little bedroom, propped up on pillows, nervously munching snacks, glad we weren't alone because, Morgan's soothing bullshit to the contrary: *It's a horror movie.*

How else do you characterize a way-too-true story about fatherhood? At least that's how we saw it.

The emperor penguins, noble, gorgeous creatures, live in the icy waters of Antarctica, feeding and frolicking and avoiding killer seals all year until it's time to mate. Why the dead of winter is the time to mate, why hundreds and hundreds of male and female penguins slither up onto the ice and waddle and slide on their bellies to some preordained mating ground miles and miles away, why after pairing off—why'd she choose him? They all look alike—and having sex on the frozen ground and she delivers an egg, why does she give it to him? Why does she get to waddle back to the water to feed—they haven't had a thing to eat since they started marching—while he and the rest of the future fathers huddle together in the howling, freezing winds, *balancing their eggs on their webbed feet?*!?!

Whywhywhywhywhy? Leonard and I muttered plaintively, shaking our heads in pity and terror, the classic Aristotelian tragic emotions, as we watched this excruciating process of mating and procreation, our horrified faces superimposed over the plight of the emperors staring back at us in the reflection of the TV screen.

What we found so moving, so disturbing, so stunningly biographical was the quiet helplessness and utter bewilderment of the emperor penguin fathers stoically hunkered down waiting for their women to return, stealing glances at the egg balanced precariously on their feet as the winter winds buffet them through the endless Antarctic night. Even though we'd seen the movie before, we were transfixed. Some movies so completely suspend your disbelief, they manage to create the pathetic hope that the rerun will somehow end differently. But our suspense had little to do with the penguins. We knew they'd endure their trials and tribulations and even fruitfully multiply, since to the best of our knowledge they were still down there in Antarctica, freezing and fucking and reproducing.

But how are Old Leonard and Old Eric going to balance their eggs on their feet?

A real horror story, we agreed.

We covered our eyes. We couldn't bear watching this part. A spaced-out, starving dad-to-be lets his mind wander for an instant to whatever emperors dream of: empress pussy, a tasty fish, a little sunshine maybe. His egg rolls off his feet and in no time at all his embryonic offspring freezes in its thin shell on the deadly ice. He can't pick it up without his empress, whoever she is. Can he even recall her penguin face?

There's a close-up of the noble beast, black and white with a fantastic accent of orange grief across his head.

"Oh my God," Leonard groaned. He'd been peeking.

His fellow emperors turn away from the emperor fuck-up. He is not so much shunned as nonexistent because the other penguins cannot bear to imagine what is going through the bereft father's mind. Of course it was ridiculous anthropomorphizing, but as Leonard and I watched the lost egg die on the ice, our own resolve stiffened.

We'll never fuck up like that!

We couldn't bear it, and not only because we detested criticism of any kind. It was worse than that.

Ohhhhhh, much worse, Old Eric.

We loved our kids.

Morgan was right. It is a love story. A tragic love story.

"I gotta pee." Leonard hit the pause button and tiptoed to the bathroom. Dazed, I got up and went to the freezer. The blast of icy air was ominous, but I managed to snatch two Popsicles.

"If I recall, the worst part is over," Leonard sighed as we settled back and hit the play button.

The mothers finally reach the far-off water, fill their bellies, march back, somehow find their mates, and retake possession of the egg in yet another excruciating dance during which more eggs are lost. The surviving chicks hatch. The moms feed them and toss the starving dads a few leftover scraps. The little penguins become strong enough, and the whole family marches back to the water together and dives in. After that, the mother and father have nothing more to do with each other, ever.

"Next year they will pick new mates and start all over," Morgan tells us with a sigh of contented approval.

"Oh God, no!" we groaned in unison. As the credits rolled, we compared our situations to the emperor penguins. Sure, we had warmer weather and better snacks, but, as Leonard succinctly put it, "All they have to do is keep their scene together for a winter and they never see 'em again. The mother or the kids!"

"An intriguing deal."

"Wanna get something to eat? I'm starved."

We shook ourselves from our Antarctic reverie and hit the town.

We told each other repeatedly that we were tough guys. Not tough guys who go around terrorizing others, at least not deliberately, but guys who are tough enough to take whatever "they" dish out. We wholeheartedly supported each other's aspirations, the perennial aspirations of a tribe not listed officially among the other tribes, strictly ex officio, the Utterly Lost Tribe of Israel, whose members have toiled for millennia as storytellers and court jesters, magicians, scribblers, singers and actors, horn players and wild-eyed seekers of truth. Buddha was one of us, a prince who abandoned his kingdom, not to mention his weeping wife with an infant in her arms, trying in his way to be free.

What a guy!

Our Zen master was a tough guy, too. He laid down a tough regime that was deliberately, arrogantly not for everyone. He eschewed anything soft, comforting, or even remotely kind and had nothing good to say about any other teacher, practice, or even his own students' efforts.

Being tough guys, we naturally chose a tough way to make a buck. Leonard could have led a kinder, gentler existence as a renowned Canadian poet and literary novelist at a time when fewer and fewer people read either poetry or literary novels. I could have built *Zero* into the leading little journal of its day. With great effort and its Zen zest, I might have attracted ten thousand readers and been a veritable whale in a tiny pond.

Instead, we opted for show business, where success is measured in units of precious metals and box office receipts gross and net. No business like show business! No business, no show! No business for anyone but tough guys with cast-iron stomachs.

Yet the sad truth was that we were as psychically vulnerable as those unreinforced brick buildings up and down the San Andreas Fault, trembling even on a good day, hopeless suckers for the myths of freedom: ultimate, provisional, even momentary. In our distracted states of mind we were in constant danger, not just from the Big One, but from all the little tremors, caught off guard by pissed-off men, women, and children sneaking up on us when our backs were turned, trying to lay us out with a well-placed blow.

Go ahead! Give it your best shot!

We took our cues in cool from black men. We had profound admiration for their uncompromising toughness, though less for their propensity to end up prematurely dead or in jail. We thought we could get away with it.

They'll never get us, Old Eric.

Worst of all we were greedy tough guys. Not only would the Kingdom of Heaven be ours, but we were deeply fascinated, in our strange, detached, deracinated way, by the Kingdom of Earth. We tried to be free, of course we did, many times, but always with a Sinatraesque insistence on *my way*. Huddled under a tree, surviving on nettles and dank rainwater, we often asked each other:

> *What were we thinking?*
> *Why didn't they tell us?*
> *They did. We weren't listening.*
> *We held our hands over our ears.*
> *We thought they were boring old men.*
> *We thought we were smarter than them.*
> *Hee hee hee.*
> *We're lucky boys.*
> *Very lucky boys.*

This incorrigible apostasy came so naturally to us. We might have gotten away with it, might have gone free— built a fire in the swamp or even hopped a tramp steamer up the Amazon, women, wine and songs and novels, sending postcards with no return address—if we hadn't become fathers.

Leonard told me more than once he never wanted a family. There was no reason for me to doubt his declaration, but he never explained why, after the birth of his first child, after adequate time had transpired to assess the conditions of life en famille, he and Suzanne had a second child.

Being a father defined his life. Right up to the end Leonard possessed, or was burdened by, a unique sense of duty. It didn't matter to him whether or not there was a God to judge him or an eternal reward for his efforts. He knew he couldn't live with himself if he fucked up as a father, especially after the union with the mother of his children shattered.

I don't recall as a young man subscribing to any particular position regarding fatherhood, except to avoid reproduction while staying as sexually active as possible, relying on a slapdash combination of condoms, consenting females' attention to regular ingestion of oral contraceptives, and mostly the goodwill of the gods.

Late one Saturday evening in our downstairs apartment at Tremaine, Susan whispered in extremely close proximity that she was recently un-contracepted, offering me the opportunity to pause and take any unilateral measures I considered necessary. I neither paused, considered, nor otherwise interrupted the act of procreation. She got pregnant that night.

I enthusiastically got involved in the project, the way I always enthusiastically get involved in projects from literary magazines to building houses, replacing a transmission on a truck or getting enlightened.

The baby project.

I attended classes. I cooked and served Susan a hundred grams of high-quality protein a day, particularly during those crucial months they told me young Samuel Martin's brain was developing the cells I hoped would function exactly like his dad's!

We were proud parents-to-be. After a decade of confounding expectations—mostly my mother's—by dropping out of Harvard to become a professional spiritual pilgrim, I was back on track. Sort of.

First, I lit out for Mexico.

∽

It was only a little late-term road trip. Actually, really late, weeks not months before Susan's scarlet-red-letter due date of flaming doom. I drove down the Baja peninsula with an old friend to a hunting lodge south of Ensenada. He hiked for miles each day while I sat on the veranda, immobilized, my mind speechless. Then we drove home.

In no time at all we were celebrating Sam's bris in the backyard at Tremaine in March 1983, as I recounted earlier. What I left out was my memory of Leonard standing on the edge of the party with an enigmatic smile very similar to the smile he gave me the first time we met at that sesshin, a smile of encouragement to join him in the arcane activity of being Roshi's student. Watching me holding my week-old son, he seemed relieved. I'd joined him in another life-threatening, daredevil enterprise—fatherhood.

Welcome aboard, bro!

He'd been paddling his leaky little rowboat all by himself for years. Now I got in and sat down beside him and we hunched over like galley slaves. In strict time to some distant beating drum, we rowed into thick, uncharted waters.

For years after his family imploded he took the kids by himself during their school vacations to theme parks, resorts, his house on the Greek island of Hydra or the one in Montreal. In January 1986 Leonard and the kids arrived at Tremaine and collapsed. Sam was not quite three, and he was delighted by the visitors. So was Susan. We spent days hanging out, eating, watching TV, and other mindless amusements.

Adam was thirteen by then, a man according to the Jews, and he was more than a bit of that. He had a broken foot or badly sprained ankle and was on crutches. One morning the fathers and sons all went out to play in the backyard. Sam stood in the driveway in front of the garage, waiting excitedly for me to roll a ball to him so he could kick it in Adam's direction. Adam swatted the ball back to Sam distractedly. He was engaged in a seemingly urgent discussion with his father.

Leonard was an ethereal being. Most of his vital energy resided above his shoulders. He resembled one of those ancient sculpted busts set on a pedestal in wealthy Roman homes, a remarkably lifelike rendition of the subject's head alone that expressed his dignitas and gravitas. Leonard's mind and heart, his essential qualities, shone so strongly through his eyes and smile and vivid expressions that you didn't notice he was otherwise barely there. Except with his kids. He was always there with his kids.

He purposefully grabbed their attention and held it. You could say it was the old soft-shoe, Leonard on another stage, but it was better than any other performance he ever gave. If you love someone, you want them to love you back. You don't try merely to entertain, amuse, or distract—those standard goals of parenting—you seek to enchant. That's the kind of father Leonard was.

He had two separate ongoing conversations, one with Adam and the other with Lorca. As the kids grew up the vocabulary naturally grew with them, but the grammar and syntax were fixed forever while they were still quite young. Neither of them ever understood the other's language with their father.

"Watch this one!" Sam yelled, trying to get Adam's attention.

Adam, a good sport, hopped over on his crutches and rolled a few to Sam before returning to the sidelines. The Cohen men's conclave grew more intense. Leonard lowered his voice, pointing to some point he was trying to make.

Adam listened intently before replying, "But Dad . . ."

∼

But Dad . . .

But Dad . . .

But Dad . . .

It was almost a musical refrain.

Adam was about sixteen when the three of us had a discussion one evening at the house in Montreal that became forever known as: *That night we argued over how to learn to drive a car,* though we could never quite recall the exact points of disagreement, or whether the argument was even about Adam's conception of how to learn to drive a car or how to play the kazoo.

It was two against one, but the one was the Original One, Adam. Leonard and I, masters of logic and persuasion, took turns like a wrestling tag team assailing his position, cajoling, berating, denigrating, ridiculing, and belittling. It was like storming the walls of Jerusalem. Our Crusade failed utterly. Adam's mind, a mind that delighted, awed, and frustrated his father, was constructed out of dependent clauses and seamless analogies, impeccable syllogisms and the most curious collection of assumptions and proofs.

"You can't change Adam's mind," Leonard finally decided ruefully, many years later. "It's a labyrinth only he can navigate. Occasionally." He said it with the curious glow of amazement and pride and quivering trepidation a father feels if he loves his son the way Leonard loved Adam.

The father had the mind of a poet, intent on compression and precision of expression, while the son was some kind of jazz essayist who reveled in catch-me-if-you-can riffs that left his father flummoxed: *Should I try to fix this or praise it?*

I learned from Leonard—though he was the first to admit it was a fine principle that he himself could rarely adhere to—that you must decide what is essential and what is merely irritating before attempting to improve your children.

~

In his late teens Adam was in a bad car wreck, though he wasn't driving. He ended up in a hospital bed in Montreal for weeks with a halo cast screwed into his skull to allow his broken neck to heal. Leonard sat at his bedside day after day, wearily calling me every few nights to praise his son's fortitude.

Over the years I became close to Adam, kind of the only uncle he had. Leonard and I visited him in New York City when he was beginning his music career, and he came to visit Susan and me in Northampton. After he moved to LA, Adam, Leonard, and I regularly sat down together to mull over the exquisite anguish of Adam's life. He listened attentively to the desperate poetry of our suggestions for his relief.

In my earliest childhood memory of my father I'm looking down at his face as he lies on his back holding me in the air above him. I'm flying! We wrestled—*roughhousing,* he called it—until I was eighteen. *Oops, you okay, Dad? Huh, you really think your rib is broken?* After that we just poked each other in passing, a few jabs and feints.

That's all I knew about being a father at the outset. Sam was tossed, bounced, tickled, held in one hand above my head, arcing through the air in slow motion as both of us yelled "BODY *SLAM!*" I bought us father-son red boxing gloves when he was two.

Pow-pow!

We entered the realm of imagination together. He was four when I stopped reading bedtime stories to him and started making them up. Soon he was making up the stories and telling them to me.

And then, and then, and then . . .

"What's Sam doing under the blanket?" his sister Sara asked, a little peeved. She was four and he was nine. She wanted to play with him in the sand at the beach but he was hunched up beneath a blanket just out of reach of the lapping waves, busy composing an epic, a mythic battle of forces that soon sprung out of his head onto a three-foot-wide roll of brown paper he methodically filled like a Chinese scroll from outer space.

I took Sam to his first piano lessons at ten, and it didn't take him long to start pounding out improvised verses of Duke Ellington's "Satin Doll" on the upright Steinway in the dining room.

"He's pretty damn good, you know?" Leonard followed Sam's work closely.

Sam started building a vast website, a multimedia branching tree on which to hang his images, stories, music, and even a nascent blog before anyone had heard the word. I always thought Sam had better chops than me, even as I dreaded him embracing a career in creativity, much less show biz. I tried to make sure he understood it was no life for a sensible fellow. I even explained the concept of a "day job." I held my breath.

"That's what we do in regard to our sons," Leonard sighed. "We hold our breath."

≈

Our daughters were something else entirely.

That morning at Tremaine back in 1986 while the boys were out in the backyard, Lorca was busy upstairs at the kitchen table, working intently in her notebook of heavy unlined paper with her drawing and coloring materials.

"That one's quite good, darling," Leonard told her after inspecting her latest creations. "So's that one."

She frowned, pointing first to one then the other. "Which one do you like more?"

"I like them both."

"You have to like one more than the other," pronounced the eleven-year-old, black-haired, dark-eyed sprite in her challenging whisper. "I hate this one." Even now, Lorca is an image in high-contrast black and white. Until she had her first child, Lorca didn't quite seem to be of this world. It was perhaps her most endearing quality to her father.

"Cheer up, darling!" he encouraged Lorca that morning and on many occasions after.

I didn't have a daughter yet so I watched in fascination as he offered to take her to an art store for a new notebook, or more colored pencils, or paint, or whatever she needed to soothe her distress. Listening to Leonard's calm, reasoned suggestions I was nearly as hypnotized as Lorca.

"Is anyone hungry? I'm starved!" he suddenly announced. We all piled into the car for a McDonald's run.

≈

Lorca was around sixteen when she returned to Tremaine and moved into the downstairs apartment we had recently moved out of. She would live there until her father died.

Who's at the door? It's Little Lorca! Come on in, darling, come on in. I'm just hanging out with Old Eric. How was your evening? Come in and tell us all about it.

It was pretty weird.

How so?

Lorca always recounted her adventures in a tone of mock bewilderment at human behavior. She was a keen observer of absurdity, including her own, though sometimes she lost her objectivity so completely it brought her father to despair.

"I never thought in a million years I'd spend my life in LA of all places," she mused to me years later. "He wouldn't let me *leave!*" she exclaimed with a look of sad delight. "I tried but then he bought the building for my store. It was bribery." She looked very much like the eleven-year-old sprite.

∼

At fourteen, my daughter Sara announced that for her next birthday she wanted me to take her on a trip to Paris. Our closeness was more than the congruency of our personalities. Sara was the product of a deliberate experiment I'd undertaken in her earliest years. With Susan's bemused approval, I endeavored to relate to my daughter the same way I'd introduced her brother to the world: with body slams, chest dancing, belly blowers, tickle fights to the death, and finally, putting the red boxing gloves on her tiny hands to answer the crucial question: *Are you a man or are you a mouse?*

We did not neglect her intellectual development. We exchanged heads, miming the unscrewing of our craniums and carefully handing them to each other, then screwing each other's head on our own neck and conversing in imitations of each other.

At about eight, I started taking her clothes shopping. Sam went clothes shopping with his mother. We all seemed fine with this arrangement. I still took her clothes shopping when she was in her twenties.

Instead of Paris I offered a trip to California for her birthday. She was only a year and a half when we moved to Northampton, and she hadn't been back since. In April 2003 we flew to LA and began our trip at Tremaine. As a kid, Sara knew Leonard from his visits to Northampton. Now at fifteen, already fearlessly independent and proficient at life, she wanted to present her grown-up self to Leonard. He gallantly appreciated her poise and her beauty.

Naturally we went clothes shopping on Melrose Avenue and dropped in at Lorca's store. That was the beginning of their friendship. Sara and I rented a car and drove north on Ventura Highway, the classic California road trip with her soundtrack playing, a mixed CD she'd put together featuring early Norah Jones. We stopped for fried artichokes in Watsonville and spent three days in San Francisco wandering around the city. She walked too fast and impatiently waited at corners for me to catch up.

A decade later we were walking down Third Avenue in New York after a dinner of Japanese delicacies, a substantial amount of beer and sake, and one of our periodic debriefings regarding the high and low points of our lives.

"You cradle robber!" someone shouted at me.

Startled, we turned to the wild-eyed, electric-haired, ill-shaven street denizen pointing at me in a fire-and-brimstone pose of accusation. "Shame on you! She's young enough to be your daughter!"

"She IS my daughter!"

My accuser's eyes widened in confusion. He blinked at me and then at Sara.

She just grinned and nodded. *Yup! That's me!*

The guy slapped his forehead. "Oh, mannnn, I'm sorry."

"Don't sweat it."

"Uh, okay. Well, take care!" He waved and ambled off.

Sara looked at me and shrugged, not at all displeased, a sophisticated acknowledgement that even if others couldn't quite understand us, we did.

"Cradle robber!" Leonard chuckled when I told him the story. "That's pretty good."

I never had to explain to him what Sara and I were about; he and Lorca were very much the same way. Our daughters appreciated our efforts on their behalf, our wholehearted empathy, our praise for all their qualities, our constant concern for their moment-to-moment well-being.

Thanks, Dad.

They couldn't thank us enough, so they thanked us again!

Thanks, Dad!

"All you're trying to do is get them to smile at you," Leonard often reminded me. He was referring to women of all shapes and sizes. In this regard our daughters were the greatest successes of our lives. Naturally it pissed off our sons, and they harbored grudges against their sisters.

"They can get away with anything."

Leonard and I were mystified by their complaint.

Come on, boys, smile!

Smile at your fathers, fountains of wisdom, you lucky lads. Drink from the waters of our hard-won experience and take to heart the lessons we're trying to pass on to you free of charge (heh-heh), no strings attached. We're not judging your efforts to be men, and even when you do fuck up (of course your sisters don't fuck up, they're just having a bit of a hard time), we're there for you, aren't we?

Leonard and I rarely glanced in the mirrors of the eyes of others, except the mirrors of the eyes of our children. Before these mirrors we primped and preened and stood up straight and tall and adjusted the crowns on our heads to appear more like the kings we hoped they saw us as.

In that way we were like every other father, hoping against hope we could somehow make it easier for our kids, smoother sailing than it had been for us.

Smile forever, you delicate creatures!

It was our deepest, most ridiculous ambition, which is saying an awful lot about two guys of our grandiosity.

There was only one pesky problem. How were we supposed to balance the fragile eggs on our feet as we huddled on the frozen tundra, patiently waiting for the little darlings to hatch and waddle off on their own two feet?

Too bad we weren't penguins.

five

BIRD ON A WIRE

GIVEN THE ENORMOUS ACCLAIM Leonard garnered when he was in his seventies, returning triumphantly in 2008 to packed theaters, arenas, and stadiums worldwide, it is easy to forget that for thirty years prior, even though he turned out eight studio albums, Leonard Cohen was stone-cold dead commercially in the US, his ghost eulogized periodically in *Rolling Stone*, revered by what became known as his "cult following."

Leonard Cohen, huh? Is he still alive?

At the end of the 1970s the music business was booming from the revenue generated by hit record albums that sold in the multimillions. Touring was an expensive means of promotion, the opposite of today when the only real money in music is in live performances. There was no need

for Leonard's label, Sony Records (née Columbia), to in-
vest in promoting him in America, since they could count
on the steady, modest sales of his albums in Canada and
Europe where he was still big. Those royalties were enough
to pay Leonard's bills.

"It adds up," he'd say thoughtfully, even though he really didn't know exactly what he spent. He left that to his
manager, Marty Machat, who was quite fond of Leonard
and gave him an Amex card and some loose blank checks
to carry around. Leonard's style of life was modest—
Tremaine was hardly a house in the Hollywood Hills—but
supporting Suzanne and his children, his constant travel,
and the various streams and small rivers that flowed to old
friends, girlfriends, and Roshi's scene did indeed add up.
Still, as long as he kept cranking out new albums and flog-
ging them with inexpensive foreign tours, he could balance the egg on top of his feet, not even webbed, but clad
in slippery old cowboy boots.

Leonard Cohen, huh, is he still alive?

In late 1984, adhering to a certain ritual, Leonard personally carried his new album, *Various Positions,* to the New
York offices of Sony to sit with the honchos who'd ad-
vanced him the money to produce it while they listened
to it for the first time. The story of that listening session
has become almost apocryphal. In his final interview with

David Remnick of the *New Yorker*, Leonard recalled the re-action of Sony president Walter Yetnikoff after hearing the new album:

Leonard, we know you're great, but we don't know if you're any good.

Sony declined to even release the album in America, much less promote it. Leonard was forced into the humil-iating task of finding an indie distributor. In the Remnick interview, Old Leonard coolly concludes the story with this quotable line about Sony, and you can practically hear his wry sarcasm: *I have always been touched by the modesty of their interest in my work.*

The unspoken punch line is that Walter Yetnikoff passed on the album that includes such iconic Leonard Cohen songs as "Dance Me to the End of Love," "If It Be Your Will," and Leonard's most covered song of all, the vir-tual anthem of his career, "Hallelujah."

That Yetnikoff! Hah! What a moron!

Except that's not the real punch line to the story.

Leonard recounted the abortive listening session with Sony to me a couple of months later in his kitchen at Tremaine. There was nothing wry or even vaguely amused in his voice as he stood behind the counter beside the sink, like the at-torney he once aspired to be for a semester at Columbia Law School, addressing his jury of one. I was mesmerized by his lurid description of the crime scene, the excessive opulence of the Sony executive suite in those halcyon days in the music industry. I nearly jumped out of my seat as Leonard ID'd the perpetrator of the crime, omitting no detail right down to the gleam of his expensive cufflinks.

Leonard was brimming with outrage.

At himself!

He knew Yetnikoff was right.

While Leonard's album may well have been *great*, greatness is for posterity. In the present tense the only thing that matters is record sales, the only definition of *good*. Walter Yetnikoff knew what a hit record sounded like, and what he heard sounded like something he could sell easily enough in Toronto and Hamburg and Paris. But risk serious money promoting it in America? Not a chance.

Leonard was smart enough to get it, even if in those days he had no idea what a hit sounded like since he rarely turned on the radio. But the Old Boy was a quick study. He confided to me with a cunning grin that he wasn't any more interested than Sony was in being merely *great*. He wanted to be *good*.

I've always been competitive. Ask my sisters. We had to stop playing cards and board games at a young age. Leonard, though, was ferocious. He hid it beneath his Canadian British Empire—*bad form, old chap*—manners, but he always kept a close eye on the careers of his contemporaries. He was fed up grinding out albums that just paid the bills, laboring beneath a thickening veil of obscurity in the only place that really mattered in the pop world, his original destination when he'd set out from Montreal in pursuit of stardom—America.

He wanted a hit. Of course he did. And so did I. By then I'd been in the movie biz long enough to know as well as he did that a hit changes everything.

Wait a minute.

Wasn't enlightenment supposed to change everything?

Unfortunately we hadn't stuck around long enough to find out. We had to exchange our beloved black Zen dresses for Marching Penguin suits and reluctantly bid Roshi good-bye, even though inside our snappy new world-beater outfits we were still the same forlorn, twice-born souls. Only now we were balancing our precious little eggs on trembling feet, trying not to starve or freeze or let anyone down, chanting our new mantra.

A hit changes everything.

From then on—except for lunch breaks during which we huddled in intense speculation about the meaning and purpose of our endeavors—we descended into the mine, rarely missing a shift, fighting our fear we'd gotten on the wrong elevator going down the wrong shaft and all we'd unearth at the bottom would be lumps of fossil fuel and not the precious metals—silver, gold, and platinum—of the hit that would change everything. Down in the depths, our sweaty shoulders bumping in the close confines, our breath shortened by the fetid dusty air, with callused palms and clanking shovels and brave faces we quietly cheered each other on and dug.

~

Just before Sam was born in 1983, I went to work for Interscope, a fledgling production company funded by Ted Field, the young heir to the Marshall Field fortune of Chicago. Interscope became a success in movies and later a megaphenomenon in the rap music industry. I was hired as a development executive/in-house writer, splitting my time between wining and dining agents and writers on a fat expense account to acquire new properties for Interscope, and rewriting scripts we already had in development.

Leonard provided the young warrior with his battle chariot, a 1967 burgundy Mercedes 220S, the two-door European coupe with a sunroof and those rare jewel headlights. It had been Suzanne's car, in storage since she moved to France with the kids.

At Interscope I was put in charge of a project aptly named *Critical Condition*, working with the original writers based in New York. It took almost three years of hard-drinking, cross-country trips, but I managed to construct a rickety shortcut in the game of Chutes and Ladders that I hoped would vault me over the other twenty-five thousand

slipping and sliding aspiring screenwriters in town, killing themselves to get a meeting with anybody who might
give them a measly development deal. Not me. I was about
to shoot a Paramount movie with my name on it—my
title was yet to be determined since I wasn't officially the
writer—directed by the highly respected Michael Apted
and starring Richard Pryor in a dramatic comeback role
after he'd nearly incinerated himself with a free-base pipe.

How could it miss?

A hit would change everything!

Meanwhile, Susan and I decided we needed to move to a
larger house in a better neighborhood if we were going to
raise a family in LA. One of the more agreeable features
of our marriage was a division of labor based on individual skills and personal inclinations whenever possible. We
cringed at other couples stumbling over each other decid-
ing whose turn it was to do what and when. For example,
I cooked and Susan cleaned up. I didn't change diapers,
though I forget precisely what I did as a trade-off, perhaps
something to do with the children's moral education. I endured an enormous amount of shit for this—admittedly a
weak pun—from every female member of my family, including my daughter Sara when she was old enough to
make judgments about her father for not changing her
diapers.

At any rate, one afternoon in early 1986 Susan, the designated house hunter, excitedly showed me pictures of a place she'd found on more than half an acre in Malibu, large enough for Susan the passionate gardener to create a small farm. It had a swimming pool, a nifty stone patio, and access to a private beach at the end of the street.

Private beach!?!

Even in 1986 dollars, at half a million it seemed like a steal. True, we were paying six hundred a month for our half of Tremaine, and we had only about a thousand bucks in the bank, but not to worry! According to our division of labor, I was the Chancellor of the Exchequer.

Leonard drove out to Malibu with Susan and me in the red Mercedes to inspect it before I left for North Carolina to shoot *Critical Condition.* We were considering the possibility of his going in on it with us. Maybe he'd take the guesthouse, a little getaway at the beach. We were both unnerved at the prospect of the Lerners leaving Tremaine.

The house was originally a Jehovah's Witness meeting hall. It had a floor-to-ceiling fireplace in the living room faced with bowling-ball-sized stones hauled up from the nearby beach. The swimming pool and Jacuzzi were homemade, too, but hey: *A swimming pool and a Jacuzzi!* From the deck of the guesthouse you could catch a glimpse of the ocean just beyond Johnny Carson's tennis court on the other side of the ravine. There was even an old horse stable I could convert into my new office. How wacky and wonderful.

We strolled down to the end of the street with a key that unlocked a massive iron gate. A magical trail of wooden steps and small bridges descended through a eucalyptus grove to Pirate's Cove, a famous, coveted surf spot beneath looming sandstone cliffs. We couldn't quite believe it.

Walking back to the car Leonard drew me aside, choosing his words carefully. "It's an amazing place, man. Little Susan would be very happy here." He'd taken to calling her by that affectionate diminutive. "I can lend you some bread to swing the deal. But . . ." The look on his face made it clear how he felt about the whole thing:

I'm worried about you, man.

Leonard cared greatly about my welfare, though I don't think he ever felt confident enough that he knew exactly what my welfare was—any more than his own—to translate his concern into specific advice.

He gingerly backed away from going in on buying the house with us. The adventure might have ended there, but luckily—good or bad I still haven't decided—it was an unprecedented moment in the history of home mortgages. Without a real job or any money in the bank, I easily refinanced Tremaine and used the cash for the down payment on the Malibu house, obtaining a liar's loan for $450,000

from a bank that would soon go under in the financial
meltdown known as the Savings and Loan Scandal.

Our variable mortgage started at 7 percent. It would
quickly rise like the mercury in a thermometer in the
Mojave Desert facing the morning sun.

~

After returning to Los Angeles from his highly informa-
tive meeting with Walter Yetnikoff, Leonard worked on
his hit-to-be with a relentless effort that would have gotten
him crowned King of the Emperor Penguins. He read me
lines, verses, and revisions. He sang me the nascent songs,
strumming a guitar at the kitchen table. He played me cas-
settes with rough mixes. Finally, I sat on a broken-down
couch in the Hollywood studio listening to him record *I'm
Your Man.*

I think it's fair to say that popular music, like all forms
of popular culture, relies on formulas, making it a science
as well as an art. Though Leonard hadn't worked from a
formula before, his intelligence was both profound and
practical. He could draw on his experience with his chemistry set from his boyhood days in Westmount.

"You did it!" I practically leapt out of my chair after
hearing the final mix of "First We Take Manhattan."

It had a pumping, churning groove propelled by a
kicking backbeat you just gotta move to. He'd taken his
lyric poetry and hammered it on the anvil of rock into

concise rhythmic compressions, fashioning the hook on which a hit either hangs or falls.

"Sony can't blow this one off," I fearlessly pronounced.

"You think so?"

He actually asked me that. As if I ever knew, then or now, what sells or not. He had a curious expression on his face, sensing the danger of his position. The helium balloon of hope had lifted his toes dangerously off terra firma.

Even though "First We Take Manhattan," "I'm Your Man," and "Tower of Song" all move you to the grooves, that wasn't what grabbed me most about the new album; I thought the songs were hysterically funny. In interviews he was sometimes asked to elaborate on his so-called political stance in "First We Take Manhattan." He always managed to deftly say very little, because it's right there in the song, wonderfully voiced by the mad female chorus cooing in response to Leonard's seemingly profound pronouncements on the state of world affairs, the ladies professing their love for his body and his spirit and his clothes.

The first time he played it for me, he looked across the kitchen table and made his extra-serious face, a slight quiver at the corners of his downturned mouth, a mime of Talmudic wisdom. I thought it was the first time he'd fully revealed in his music the mordant humor that permeated his poetry and fiction and his life. Like the little laughing

skeleton effigies of the Mexican Day of the Dead that sat
on the windowsill in the kitchen, there was Old Leonard
in a sombrero and shiny black boots and silver belt, wail-
ing to a mariachi band.

Sounds like a hit?

Maybe.

~

"What a revolting development," Leonard sighed, quoting
Daffy Duck of cartoon fame. He cut a distinguished figure as a hospital visitor in his dark gray suit and tie and a
hat, which he removed and placed on the windowsill beside the small bouquet of flowers he'd purchased in the
gift shop downstairs. Pulling up a chair beside my bed, he
peered through my morphine haze.

In the summer of 1987 back surgery required a surgical cut through the muscles and a five-day hospital recovery. The surgeon was pleased. He'd found the culprit that
had eluded the CT scan—this was right before MRIs—a
completely torn disc compressing two nerve roots. He'd
removed it, and now, he assured me, I would be fine.

"How's Little Susan doing?" Leonard inquired discreetly.

That was more complicated than my recent surgical
procedure.

Susan and I had moved into our new house on the aptly
named Point Dume in Malibu a year before, in June 1986,
right after I returned from shooting *Critical Condition*. As
we pulled up to our new digs in a rental truck—thanks to

the giddy bank we could afford a half-million-dollar house but not professional movers—an underground sprinkler in the homemade circular drive ruptured, as my disc soon would, and a geyser shot up near the front door. Such omens are ignored at great peril, but I was bursting with the false confidence engendered by viewing a movie on the set in daily parts surrounded by actors and crew cheering their own efforts.

Not long after we unpacked in Malibu, Paramount took a quick look at the director's first cut and fired me. They hired a famous team of jokesters and reshot a bunch of idiotic trash on the studio lot in LA, attempting to retrofit the movie into the slapstick comedy they thought they'd paid for. Richard Pryor had no choice but to take pratfalls on command. The finished product was a dismal hash. Susan and I viewed it at the local theater in Malibu. It was painful to watch, in no small part because I'd recently blown out my back in a pick-up basketball game at the gym of the Malibu elementary school. I could barely sit through the coming attractions.

I was unemployed and the mortgage had already jumped to 8.5 percent. Susan was six months pregnant. My knee buckled crossing a street in traffic while I held Sam's hand and I fell at his little feet. I went in for surgery.

～

"Do me a favor?" I asked Leonard.

"Of course." He rose from the bedside chair.

"Could you use your considerable charm to lure a nurse in here with another shot of morphine? They're sadistic about waiting the full four hours, except it wears off after three and a half."

"Say no more, bro."

He soon waved from the doorway as Nurse Ratched, thoroughly annoyed, strode up to my bed with a dripping syringe. I bared my poor black-and-blue, needle-punctured ass, and thrust it longingly at her.

Seeing the renewed sparkle in my eye, Leonard sat back down and pulled his chair closer. We listened to the purr of the bed motor elevating me even higher.

"Is the album completely finished?" I asked.

Although Leonard often shook his head at certain of his contemporaries who spent inordinate amounts of time in the recording studio—*Getting background bird noises just right*—he was nevertheless his own kind of meticulous perfectionist, not only in the matter of his lyrics but in every aspect of the production and postproduction of an album. *I'm Your Man* was no exception.

At first he dismissed my inquiry with a shrug, as if at a time like this there was no need to get into it, but I knew he was just being polite. He was eager to bring me up to date.

"It's nearly done," he whispered. "There are just a few details left . . ." He hesitated, as if suddenly remembering a few details he might have forgotten.

"Congratulations," the morphine sighed, absolutely certain how wonderful everything was going to be.

"Thank you."

"And then?"

"Well, you know, the pilgrimage to Sony."

"Ah."

"That pesky little detail."

"Right."

For the past three years we'd marched side by side as designated witnesses to each other's labors, roles we continued to play in each other's lives until the end. It was an endlessly hair-raising tale, not for the faint of heart, not for Susan, who after a while froze at the sound of the telephone ringing. For some ridiculous reason I kept assaulting her with accounts of my deals, my projects, the mishaps and momentary misshapen hopes, when I didn't need to say anything to her because I was going to tell all of it to Leonard. *Guess what happened at the office today?*

He didn't have a wife. I have no idea what, if anything, he told the various women who passed through his life. I think he tried to report on his efforts to Suzanne. After that he wised up and shut up and saved it for me. No one else wanted to hear us bitch about our work, which is curious, because everyone else bitches about their work, but as Leonard noted, "They don't think we work. They think we're having fun."

It annoyed us like a persistent itch. We were denied the right to bitch about our work because in their eyes (*them* being everyone except ourselves) our problems were of our own creation. Well, whose aren't? But somehow if you are a doctor, or a lawyer, or a teacher, or an executive, even though you chose your profession, it was a responsible choice, a choice in harmony with the established order—moral, social, economic, and Jewish. Whereas the members of our subversive tribe choose chaos and rebellion. It was sad. A bit pathetic, too. Even though we insisted on thumbing our noses at them, we still hoped for a little more than the cold shoulder.

Take your bitching outside and howl at the moon 'cause we don't want to hear it at the dinner table.

After Leonard finished his report, as per our protocol, he asked for mine. "So where are you with your project?"

My *project*, the solution to my pesky problems of a rising mortgage, screaming pain, and a second child on the way, was a Hail Mary pass with the clock running out. I was writing a spec script, a script no one was paying me for, not a shoot-'em-up, knock-'em-down, sidesplitting outer-space box office bonanza, but an indie-type *film* about a guy whose identity is taken away from him. A noirish tale. With a girl of course.

Leonard had followed its progress closely. "Is the end in sight?" he asked hopefully.

"Depends on the angle you're tilted."

"It usually does," he sighed. "Gotta run, man. I'll come back soon." He stood up and put his hat on. "How long till they let you out of here?"

"Supposed to stay until Friday, but I'm thinking of checking out tomorrow. I hate begging for drugs."

"It's particularly humiliating."

"I've got a few Percocets at home."

"Always prepared. Have you settled on the title yet?" he asked.

"Bird on a Wire."

"Catchy."

six

THE MAYFLOWER

I NEVER KNEW THAT other guy, the one who chased down a very particular version of fame that he defined for himself: literate but with crowd appeal, the poet and rock star combined, the guy who immortalized in song his residency at the Headquarters of Warhol Hip in the sixties, the Chelsea Hotel. Over the years I caught a few glimpses of that guy in old documentaries, the wide-eyed boy hungry for adulation and girls, though a tad nervous about it all, but I didn't recognize him.

Leonard was living at the Chateau Marmont in LA when I met him, even hipper in the seventies than the Chelsea Hotel in New York. A vampiric voice at the front desk answered the phone demanding to know to whom you wished to speak. No one knew exactly what went on in

the exclusive bungalows behind the mysterious castle overlooking Sunset Boulevard until March 1982 when everyone in the world knew, after John Belushi overdosed and
his celebrity friends fled into the night.

Leonard had moved into our house on Tremaine by
then. As much as its proximity to Roshi's zendo, its obscure location suited his newfound interest in anonymity.
He chose his restaurants carefully. He didn't mind if a fan
respectfully approached to whisper appreciation for his
work—fans were strangers—as long as he didn't run into
someone he might have known, an interaction demanding the presentation of a persona that increasingly held
little interest for him.

That's why he changed hotels in New York.

It was his third city after Montreal and Los Angeles.
For a time his kids lived in New York with Suzanne. His sister, Esther, his only sibling, lived on the Upper West Side.
Until they tore the place down in 2004, whenever he came
to town Leonard stayed at the Mayflower Hotel.

It was located on Central Park West, just above Columbus Circle, facing the southwest corner of the park. From
the windows on the upper floors you could see over the
treetops the iconic grande dames: the Plaza, Park Lane,
Pierre, Sherry-Netherland, Carlyle, and St. Regis, hotels
where I stayed while I worked for Interscope on *Critical
Condition* in the mideighties.

The lobby of the Mayflower was a bleak, cavernous
space resembling the waiting room of a bus terminal. In-

deed, busloads of packaged tourists arrived and departed regularly, pushing past each other, led by old bellmen dragging flimsy, overloaded luggage trolleys through the flapping doors, creating a wind tunnel that only added to the chaos of the lobby. There was no place to sit and see or be seen. The front desk was usually crowded with guests waving city street maps. The Mayflower had 365 rooms in two eighteen-floor towers.

On my first trip to New York in the fall of 1983, I phoned Leonard at the Mayflower as soon as I was ensconced in my suite at the St. Regis.

"You made it!" he cheerfully exclaimed. "What are your plans? Wanna fall by?"

My first meeting wasn't until the next day, so I grabbed my coat and walked across Central Park South, inhaling the smell of autumn leaves and the horseshit of the harnessed beasts that hauled tourists around in the carriages lined up at the entrance to the park.

"It's terrific, eh?" Leonard sang the praises of his accommodations, welcoming me into his huge suite, furnished in the style now known as "midcentury." The charmless, institutional gray and green angular furniture was in dire need of reupholstery, radiating a patina of exhaustion that harmonized perfectly with Leonard's own patina in those days.

"It's practically as big as Tremaine!" He proudly showed me a kitchen of sorts, hinting at long-term residence. It had a sink, a couple of plates and silverware in a cupboard, a toaster, and a small fridge, though no stove to actually cook. The suite's most impressive feature by far was the massive king-size bed with enormous pillows and a comforter that would comfort anybody. The bathroom was decades overdue for an update. The ill-fitting plastic shower curtain didn't really keep all the intermittent hot water inside the stall, and the tiny sink had no place to put anything. Then there was the Mayflower's notorious room service: awful food ridiculously slow in arriving.

All of which was beside the point. The Mayflower's real virtue for Leonard was its invisibility on any map of the stars, terrestrial or celestial. It was the perfect place to disappear in the middle of New York City.

Despite the questioning looks I got from my movie industry colleagues during my brief tenure as a semi-suit, I began staying at the Mayflower, too, timing my trips to New York City whenever possible to coincide with Leonard being there.

In 1989 Susan and I moved back east to Northampton, Massachusetts, an easy three-hour drive to the curb in front of the hotel, where a bellman greeted me familiarly, whisking my car off to some hidden parking locale for a few days.

It was nearly impossible to pick up a check in Leonard's presence, and he always insisted on making my reservation and putting it on his bill, citing the amusing rationale that we weren't merely hanging out and having a good time, it was work. According to him I was providing valuable assistance in a particularly difficult but necessary endeavor.

Leonard's sister Esther was a warm, brassy, bleached-blond Orthodox-temple-going Jew, a wacky creature who loved her brother very much and was beloved by him. I first met Esther shortly after we moved into Tremaine. She and her husband, Victor, an even wackier character, regularly came out to visit. Leonard described Victor as being *in the frequent-flyer business.* He'd been in finance, but after retiring he and Esther traveled relentlessly, not primarily in pursuit of destinations but rather the accumulation of mileage points. Victor often booked ridiculous legs of complicated routes to places they didn't even want to go, but in those days Esther was easily amused. I quite loved her and she took a shine to Susan and young Sam. They came to LA even if Leonard wasn't in town and stayed upstairs.

After we moved out to Malibu, Leonard converted the garage into a guest apartment for her. After Victor died, though, Esther began a long battle with cancer, and her visits became less frequent. Instead, he visited her in New York City. The Mayflower wasn't far from her apartment. She wanted him to give her as much time as she felt she deserved whenenver he was in New York, but the problem

was that Esther had the ability to render her brother instantly cross-eyed.

    I gotta spend time with Esther. I really could use a hand, Old
Eric.

∼

In general, Leonard's interest in food was perfunctory. He
sometimes sighed, "I wouldn't eat, you know, if it weren't
absolutely necessary." A meal for him was more about the
social experience than the digestive one, but a very particular social experience. He liked to assemble odd config-
urations of his children, girlfriend at the time, manager,
personal assistant—*Let's all meet up at the restaurant*—in a
public gathering with firm boundaries on behavior and
intimacy so he could play the gracious host at a slight remove, at the head of the table, smiling as the crosscurrents
of conversation insulated him from full participation.

    He experienced a pleasant warmth from this nonspe-
cific human company. *Let's order some of those, oh, plenty of*
those, they're terrific, and some of those for you, darling, I know
you like them, and a plate of these. He preferred to regularly
patronize a few remarkably untrendy restaurants where
the staff doted on him in a reserved, old-world way.

    In the course of forty years there were only rare occa-
sions that Leonard and I went out to eat, just the two of
us—maybe an occasional breakfast—as if we didn't want
to dilute our time together. Hence a lifetime of snacking.

Upon my arrival at the Mayflower, we would walk to the nearby Gristedes market to lay in supplies: Hebrew National salamis, chopped liver, fish pâtés, cheeses, crackers, cans of salted nuts, pickles, and a rotisserie chicken. On our way back to the hotel we stopped at the liquor store for wine and something more fortifying.

Sometimes, if only to stretch our legs and get a bit of fresh air, we ate outside the comforting confines of the hotel, though we usually got no farther than the line of food carts around the corner above Columbus Circle. The curbside offerings multiplied and diversified over the years, but Leonard stuck to his hot dog from the iconic Sabrett cart with the umbrella. Few items of food excited him as much as a good hot dog, over which he could wax poetic. I suspect it was another Jewish thing. He once told me that the all-beef hot dog was created because the European Jewish immigrants wouldn't touch the pork sausages popular at the time of their arrival. He was quite proud that the hot dog had become an all-American staple like bagels.

I would start with one to be sociable, and then continue down the line of mobile food emporiums. "You're a big guy. You need a lot of sustenance," he noted, waiting patiently while I polished off a lamb gyro with white sauce and then an Italian sausage with peppers and onions for a finale.

∾

Feeding ourselves wasn't the problem; it was dinner with Esther that loomed, the event he needed my help in pulling off. It took several phone calls to negotiate the venue. She always wanted him to come uptown to her apartment, pick her up, and take her out to a proper restaurant, just the two of them. It wasn't an unreasonable request, but it was beyond Leonard's capacities. Inevitably he wore her down until she agreed to come to the hotel for dinner.

"Eric's in town. He'll join us, okay? Of course, you love Eric!"

As a concession, he'd tell her to arrive early and come up to his room so we could relax and hang out. We'd race back to Gristedes and collect the fixings for an elegant paper-plate spread of choice hors d'oeuvres, kosher items and rare treats from dusty jars hidden on the market's highest shelves.

She would usually show up around five, dressed in timelessly fashionable good taste. Leonard took her coat and scarf and hung them in the closet, then ushered her into the living room, where we'd laid out our offerings. She took a quick glance and shrugged, remaining standing despite our entreaties for her to take a seat.

"Try the chopped liver, Esther. It's not bad."

Though her hands might hover over the tasty morsels like discerning hawks, she never tried anything. "I'm not hungry."

She'd ask him how he was, how Lorca and Adam were doing. She'd report on her recent phone conversations with Lorca, with whom she was very close. I want to make sure I get the tone right, because so far it sounds quite awful. It was more complicated than that. A lot of affection also filled the room. Esther had a droll wit. You were never quite sure if she was making a joke, or a cutting comment, or just some batty observation, though she wasn't all that batty, usually right on point. She was, after all, Leonard's sister.

I engaged her in conversation. That was my role as backup in this operation. Esther was genuinely interested in how my life was going. I could tell her anything and she was empathetic to my trials and tribulations. But she wasn't my sister. Leonard resisted her efforts to pry information out of him about his life, unwilling to make it available for her comment, or worse, her approval.

"The wine is really good, Esther, you should try some," he suggested. She accepted only if I poured a glass for her.

We took the elevator downstairs for dinner. In the invariably empty hotel dining room, a jacketed waiter presented us with our oversized, leather-clad menus. Esther put on her reading glasses and ducked out of sight behind hers, intently perusing the offerings, until the waiter reappeared and stood beside her, pad at the ready.

"Madame?"

She didn't respond.

Leonard smiled. So far all was going according to the script. I made my choice, then Leonard ordered his customary lamb chops, "Well done, burnt if possible."

Finally, with a great sigh, Esther laid down her menu and declared, "Nothing for me."

We said nothing, as if her refusal to order anything to eat at dinner was in no way out of the ordinary, much less an indication of even her slightest displeasure.

Even though it was the same play we'd played for years, the one Leonard and I rehearsed before her arrival, this moment was pregnant with suspense. Would there be a sudden deviation from the script?

Leonard and I smiled and made small talk with Esther until our meals arrived. We tucked in and inhaled the aroma of our dinners. We kept smiling as Esther raised her knife and fork like gladiatorial weapons and stabbed bits and bites off our plates, nibbling them quickly, impatiently fending off Leonard's offers to call the waiter back so she could order something for herself.

"I'm not hungry," she insisted between mouthfuls of his burnt lamb chops and my medium-rare rib eye.

After many years, Leonard and I decided to change the script anyway. I ordered two dinners for myself and slid plates to her without comment.

~

"I love Esther," Leonard insisted at the outset of our debriefing after putting Esther in a taxi home.

"Of course you do." It was beyond dispute. "So do I."

"Esther is terrific!" Leonard enthused.

"She's terrific!" I enthused.

"But she's horrible to me!"

I sighed. It was impossible to argue with that. At least in these particular circumstances.

"I have no idea what her case is against me, Old Eric. Do you?"

For a long time neither of us had a clue. Then it finally began to dawn on us.

~

I met Suzanne, the mother of Leonard's children, for the first time one evening in 1984. For several years he'd hauled his ass to the French countryside, sleeping in a trailer outside the house he bought for Suzanne so he could spend time with his kids, until she sold the place and moved back to America. Now they were living in a brownstone in New York City in the Village.

We took a cab downtown from the Mayflower to entertain Adam and Lorca while Suzanne went out for the evening. Adventures in babysitting, as the title of a popular movie of the day might call it.

The apartment was dark, seemingly windowless. Leonard and I sat uncomfortably on a low couch, the kids darting around like mice, anticipating, as we were, Suzanne's dramatic entrance. She didn't disappoint. She was a compelling presence: delicate catlike frame, black hair and porcelain-white skin, and eyes the size of saucers, huge portals into the original universe just before the big bang. A female friend of similar modality accompanied her, both of them dressed head to toe in black.

Leonard and I rose like the gentlemen we were and introductions were made. Suzanne barely acknowledged me on her way out with her friend. Leonard and I took the kids to eat at some tacky place with harsh fluorescent lights. It was dismal. The encounter with Suzanne had immobilized him like a stun gun to the chest. I wasn't surprised, prepped for the encounter since that day I accompanied him up to Woodrow Wilson Drive to retrieve his belongings in cardboard boxes and inspect the scene of the disaster. In the years since, he'd presented me with numerous new pieces of evidence in his case against her.

Despite the modern state of family law in America, there is really no such thing as no-fault divorce, at least not in the dazed, squinting eyes of the combatants, all rumors of *amicable* to the contrary. Every divorced person I've ever known, male or female, after being denied the opportunity to make their case in a public court of law, becomes determined to prove beyond a doubt that *the fault* was entirely their ex's in the only court left to them, the court of friendship.

You have to take your friend's side. You can't question their charges, evidence, or verdict. You can't even hint it would be better for their health to *move on*, or any other sensible nonsense. That night, as Leonard intended, I'd seen it for myself, in lurid black-and-white, like Peeping Tom photos shot by a sleazy private eye hired to document the outrage, to establish beyond all doubt who had done who wrong. It was perfectly clear—wasn't it?—why he was sprawled in a plastic chair, head in hands, his junk food barely picked at, his children morose.

Cheer up, Old Dad!

Around the corner from the front desk of the Mayflower Hotel was a breakfast and lunch café, renovated in the fern-y style of the seventies with blond wood and too-shiny brass. The tables were set beside a wall of glass that looked out upon Central Park. A waist-high partition separated the café from the Mayflower's bar. It had a dozen rarely occupied stools. Anyone who wandered in was usually killing time before heading out for more promising destinations, unlike Leonard and me, for whom the Mayflower bar fulfilled all our promises.

Real bars weren't easy to find in Los Angeles, or even in New York anymore. They'd been suddenly transformed into hot spots for arranging sexual adventures with total strangers, or loud venues for watching sports on television, neither activity, in our opinion, appropriate to a bar's true purpose as a place of serious contemplation, not all that different from a zendo.

Sitting on a high stool with your elbows resting lightly on the counter, your precise, slightly hunched posture is as important as the perfectly erect spine in zazen. You gaze with slightly hooded lids at the entire cosmos displayed before you in neatly bottled rows. You lower your eyes into the refracted light from the liquid and cubes in your glass. The prowling bartender is your jikijitsu, the zendo master. He knows exactly when to reinvigorate you with a refill.

Like zazen, it is best not to practice alone at a bar. That's pagan. But unlike the zendo, you don't want to practice with a group surrounding you. Even three is too many, forcing you to either swivel back and forth if you're in the middle or lean out of posture to make contact with the other end of the trio.

Two is the correct number.

No one else ever joined us at the bar at the Mayflower to disturb our dialogue, voices low with only the occasional tilting of chins or raising of eyebrows for emphasis, keeping our conversations private. You can't find privacy like that anywhere else. Not even in the kitchen at Tremaine. The walls had ears. Sandra the wonderful housekeeper bustled through the kitchen all morning—it seemed like every morning but it was probably only twice a week, which was once more than really needed to wash and fold the Old Boy's underwear and vacuum dust that wasn't there; he was too generous and fond of Sandra to cut her hours back—and other people might actually drop by. Even if they rarely did, they might.

Taking our seats at the Mayflower bar in the late afternoon or after dinner, we were quietly greeted by one of the
longtime bartenders. "Mr. Cohen, nice to see you again."

While they might have heard who *Mr. Cohen* once was,
they made no fuss about it. We were appreciated for our
generous tips, our enthusiasm for the meager snacks of tiny
pretzels and Planters peanuts, and the austerity of our re-
quests for nothing more complicated than vodka-and-some-
thing for him and Jack Daniel's on the rocks for me.

After we dropped the kids back at Suzanne's apartment that
night, we headed straight for the bar. In a raw, wounded,
harmonic minor key, the one that resonates with overtones
of klezmer, he recounted the entire evening, accurate in
detail down to the ladies' appearance: *Like a pair of perfect
assassins.*

I waited patiently until he was finished before asking
the painfully obvious question, "So, you still want to fuck
her, huh?"

I never would have asked him that question in the
kitchen of Tremaine, where Suzanne existed only as a hypothetical demon, but we were at the Mayflower bar where
the question could not be avoided.

"Of course I do." Leonard drained his glass. I cleared
my throat to attract the attention of our trusty friend who
had his back discreetly turned to us, washing and drying
glasses that hadn't even been used.

Refills appeared as if he had them at the ready.

We had a starting point for our investigation of this tricky situation. It wasn't a question of whether what Leonard wanted regarding Suzanne was good or bad, wise or insane, practical or pathetic. The burning question now facing us was whether his desire to fuck the mother of his children—recall, as I did, all the painful evidence he'd presented to me to justify his animus toward her—was the result of some real, albeit tortured attraction to her, or was instead the result of some real, albeit tortured defect of his mind, or none of the above, but rather the result of some real, albeit tortured cosmic machinery we'd yet to fully diagram.

Most mystic masters consider human desires to be impediments on the path to Liberation. Our boy Joshu Sasaki Roshi, however, embraced the personal drama of life in all its glorious, messy, contentious forms. Rather than pointing an accusing finger at the ego as the enemy of enlightenment, Roshi insisted that absolute self and limited self are inextricably linked, part and parcel of the function of zero, the ceaseless activity of the cosmos.

The only self that we can actually affirm is this self-activity that is the function of zero.

Remember?

In the austerity of the sanzen room, Roshi made the nature of absolute self clearer than any text, any talk, any other teaching possibly could. He dispensed with words, thoughts, and concepts as he engaged us in realizing absolute self. But even if you came up to Mt. Baldy and sat and marched in unison, even if you shaved your head and he gave you a monk's name and no one called you John or Harry or Marybeth anymore, you still had to comprehend the nature of the particular self you thought you'd renounced. Otherwise you had no idea what Roshi was going on about.

The bar at the Mayflower was a better place even than Baldy to conduct an arduous examination into the nature of our oh-so-limited selves. Maintaining our rigorous postures, we told each other stories that we hoped might contain little nuggets of wisdom—well, that would be asking a lot; we'd settle for tiny clues—anything that might shed a ray or two of illumination on this mystery, like Leonard's story of how he met Suzanne for the first time.

"I was at a Scientology meeting in New York City. There were all these tables to sign up for different trainings. She was standing at one of the tables with her back to me, and she leaned over to fill out the forms. You know how short skirts were in those days. I was completely captivated by the sight of her ass. I didn't even see her face. Just her ass."

The first time Leonard told me the story, he provided no commentary. It was early in our friendship, and we were still determining what we needed to explain to each other. He related this cryptic tale with a look of mimed

incomprehension, wanting to know if I had any idea what
he was talking about.

Of course I did.

"Susan was up on an eight-foot ladder as I walked into
the room. A friend had brought me there to meet her.
She was busy painting a wall, and her back was to me. She
was wearing those cutoff blue-jean shorts of the era and
flip-flop sandals. I couldn't see her face. Similar to your
situation. I was deeply impressed by the thick cascade of
multihued hair that came all the way down to her very perfect ass, which, because she was standing on a ladder, was
at my eye level."

These stories led us to revise our understanding of
"love at first sight," which, I found out years later, was what
the ancients referred to as "Cupid's arrow," except *cupido*
in Latin means *desire*, not *love*.

We peered into our nearly empty glasses and sucked
out the remains. Leonard lifted a finger in the direction of
the bartender, who was now standing at attention at the far
end of his domain. "Could we have another round when
you get a chance?"

"Certainly, Mr. Cohen."

Did we have any idea what we were doing? We didn't
preface our stories with *Oh, here's another good one about
my limited self*. We repeated the same stories to each other
over time, not forgetting we'd told them before. We
thought they were worth telling again because the stories

changed—not the events or the details, but the point of view—and in each retelling the guy in the story became someone else, someone we knew better than we did the last time we told the story.

Check this out, man, he'd begin. Whether it was brand-new or a many-told tale, he recited it with the controlled cadence of the poet and the singer. My recitations were more animated, punctuated by his murmured asides, encouragements actually, because he enjoyed the high drama I injected, while he provided the backup vocals:

Well, of course she blames you.

Pretty much standard operating procedure.

What else is new?

You'd think they might let you off the hook for a minute or two.

Are you kidding me?

We were like a pair of jewel thieves, donning leather gloves and sock hats, splitting up and heading off into the night, then meeting up later at the designated rendezvous to dump the contents of our pillowcases on the bar, oohing and aahing over all that loot.

We didn't tell these stories to reveal ourselves more fully to each other. We weren't trying to create the feeling: *Oh. How wonderful that someone else knows me as I supposedly know myself.* Quite the opposite. We reveled in our bafflement: *Who the hell are those poor guys L. Cohen and E. Lerner?*

We were writers after all, constrained in our working lives by the demands of the song, the script, the novel. Though we did our best to cram into them as much as they could hold and still sell, we had pockets full of ripe fruit left over, aching to be squeezed into an elixir that could quench our thirst.

At the bar of the Mayflower we distilled the juice into words we didn't have to share with anyone else. It was our lifelong collaboration. We had no idea whether it had anything to do with Roshi's prescription for understanding the nature of the limited self from the perspective of absolute self. It was our take. That's all.

~

That night in Suzanne's loft.

Soho was not yet the theme-park street mall of today. Suzanne and the kids had moved from the Village into a loft near the Bowery. Leonard and I emerged from the old freight elevator into the huge, newly converted industrial space, and we were greeted by someone I'd never met before, though she seemed to know me: *Oh, hello, Eric, how are you?* Suzanne's hair was pulled back, her eyes were clear, her expression touching, and her voice warmly domestic as she and Leonard went over the details of the care of their children that evening while she went out, alone this time.

We watched videos and played games with the kids. Sometime during the evening Leonard answered the phone.

After the call he muttered with odd cheer, "She said there are sheets in the closet." He made up the spare bed for himself and the pullout couch for me. That's where we spent the night.

I awoke to the aroma of strong coffee and the murmuring of adults beneath the clatter of early-morning children.

"Croissants, Eric? Or I could make some eggs."

There we were, the Cohen family and me, enjoying an elaborate formal breakfast with cloth napkins and French silverware with the Bakelite handles, Mrs. Cohen fussing over Mr. Cohen. He seemed to quite enjoy her attentions, her hand brushing his as she poured him more coffee, a helpless look on his face.

Whether moments like this occurred in their years of cohabitation, that night in Suzanne's loft completely changes the story, doesn't it?

Or does it?

~

Not that long after we bought the house on Tremaine, Leonard met the best woman he would ever encounter, Dominique Isserman. It made me feel good just to be around them. Dominique's sandy hair and sandy voice and slightly out-of-this-world earthiness reminded me of Susan. I think I was slightly in love with her. I have an indelible memory of Leonard and Dominique at Sam's bris, leaning languidly against each other, their expressions reflective of some deep understanding, not speaking so much as murmuring, mostly in French, then switching suddenly to English if I addressed them. It's a cliché, I know, but she was not just his lover; she was his friend. She was the only deeply confident woman he was ever with, a brilliant photographer, her career taking off then in that particular Parisian firmament of art/fashion/intellectual circles, though she didn't portray herself as a star. She possessed an inquisitive and sharply observant mind and a wry sense of humor.

His smile when he looked at her was a smile I never saw him give another woman. After they split up in the mideighties, he was the most ripped apart I'd ever seen him. He tried to explain why.

She wouldn't, couldn't, and shouldn't move to LA for him.

He wouldn't, couldn't, and shouldn't move to Paris for her.

It made no sense. Was it all a logistical problem?

He kept using the word *impossible*. The word took on a special meaning for us, a category of difficulty beyond all others.

Why hadn't it been Dominique leaning over that Scientology table instead of Suzanne?

∼

Less than a year after *That night in Suzanne's loft,* she filed suit against him in New York.

"She wants everything," he reported.

"I thought you already gave her everything."

"So did I."

At one point, Leonard recounted, the family court judge asked Suzanne, "Mrs. Cohen, have you considered getting a job?"

The judge's question was a pyrrhic victory.

It was as if a blacksmith took his tongs and lifted Leonard's brain out of his skull, heated it over bellowed coals, held it steady on the anvil of Leonard's desire, and hammered it into an ornament, a memento he carried with him forever, reminding him how he'd wanted to fuck the mother of his children when she no longer wanted to fuck him.

There's a statute of limitations on how long you can sit at a bar. We'd sometimes go out for walks, managing to make it all the way across the broad expanse of Central Park West, dodging speeding gypsy cabs to sit on a bench with our backs to the low stone wall that bounded the vast green space we rarely entered. Occasionally we wandered south past Carnegie Hall, where he did a few shows in the eighties, for a sandwich at the Carnegie Deli, lingering over our pickles and cream sodas until darkness fell and the hookers came out on Sixth Ave.

"They're the most beautiful women I've ever seen," he repeated several times as we slowed our pace, dazed and dazzled.

"They can't really be hookers."

"They must be runway models, taking in the night air."

"Or runaway Russian princesses."

"Hanging out in front of expensive hotels just to smile at us?"

"Should we ask one of them, or two, if they'd like to come back to the Mayflower with us?"

"What would we do with them that wouldn't make us appear pitiful?"

"I haven't a clue."

Hookers would always intrigue us that way, and in the eighties, the women who stood boldly on the sidewalk in the neighborhood of New York's finest hotels were really that beautiful, and beautifully dressed, beautifully made up, Angels of the Night who appeared as blessed apparitions to us.

And then they were gone. *Poof!* Maybe by order of a new mayor swept into office on an anti-vice campaign that had escaped our notice?

"Where'd they go?"

"Inside?"

"Inside where?"

It remained a mystery to us. One of many.

One afternoon Leonard waited for me at the bar while I waved from the curb in front of the hotel as a cab pulled away, taking an old friend of mine down to Penn Station to catch a train home to Washington, DC.

She and I had met unexpectedly years before, a meeting of hearts neither of us knew what to do with, a dangling preposition whose object we didn't question.

"I confess," Leonard confessed, choosing his words carefully as my drink arrived. "I didn't think it was a good idea when you first told me about her."

I must have frowned.

"I was worried you'd blow your scene at home."

"That isn't my intention."

He smiled wryly. "It never is."

I shrugged uncomfortably.

"But I get it now." Leonard sipped his drink and pondered this new development. "I had to see it for myself. You know?"

"I know." The way I had to see him and Suzanne.

"It's necessary for you," he finally concluded.

This is what our inquiry into the nature of our oh-so-limited selves had finally revealed: what was necessary for each of us to make a go of it.

Perhaps religion could have guided us through this vale of tears, this illusionary delusion, parted the Red Sea and given us commandments of God to live upright lives. But that wasn't what Leonard's Judaism was about, and Roshi was quite clear on this point. He didn't care if you practiced a religion, any religion, as long as you didn't ask him to give you a religion to practice.

You are a baby in a big body. Don't ask me what to do. Figure it out yourself.

So we cobbled together our own arbitrary code of conduct and never recommended it to anyone else. We weren't that vain. We made a pledge to the Unseen Powers to stand upright and bitch only to each other as we strove to support our children and the mothers of our children, giving them everything we could dredge from our wounded hearts and shaky minds, withholding only what we required for our own sustenance so we wouldn't bleed ourselves dry, killing the Golden Geese and letting everyone down.

Our long-term project, of course, was that elusive second birth of Dr. James that would somehow complete our incomplete psyches and fill the gaping holes through which the wind howled even on a sunny day in June. In the meantime, though—once we came to terms with the distinct possibility that this *meantime* (very mean time indeed) might last quite a while—we needed temporary patches, tarpaulins, sandbags, at least a fucking umbrella to shield us from the piercing gusts battering our tender neural tissues.

A much better solution would have been to get out of the wind, but we couldn't make a run for it, right? We had our code of conduct. We had to keep the machinery up and running so we could crank out those clever phrases and witty rhymes that kept everyone, if not deliriously happy, then at least fed, shod, housed, and walking around with a little change in their pockets.

That's why it was up to us, our duty even, to decide what was necessary for our own survival and weather all storms of recrimination for our decisions.

I don't feel compelled to enumerate all of my adventures in necessity since the age of fourteen. I think it sufficient to report that I managed to hew a path of my own, picking up a degree from Harvard, garnering a few screen credits, buying a few houses and paying a few mortgages, sending my kids through college, loving and caring for them along the way, showing up as a son and brother, and doing the best I could as a husband. Meanwhile, I was simultaneously hopping, skipping, and jumping through a parallel universe, a career in recklessness, not the tawdry one of abusing substances, but still dancing close to the line that demarcates the perils of misadventures.

Leonard had his own necessities.

Not long after he and Dominique broke up, Leonard confided to me at the Mayflower bar that he'd given a lot of thought to it and had decided: *I'm off fucking.*

He took a few nibbles of tiny pretzels and a long swallow of his vodka and glanced at me to see if I had any clue as to what he was even talking about. I didn't then. I was thirty-five years old and more interested in fucking than pretty much anything else. But he wasn't talking about sex. There would be more of that in his life, though never in the same way. He'd come to a kind of existential understanding of the difference between sex and fucking.

Real fucking.

"I can't do it again."

Leonard was talking about the interpenetration of lives that happens when real fucking takes places. He was talking about the creation of a family. That's what he couldn't do again, because he already had a family. He would continue to rail against Suzanne, but she was the mother of his children. Even when he filled her role and became mother and father to his kids, he wouldn't replace her with another woman. There would never be another mother of his children, or another mother of other children he would father. That's what he was *off of.* True to his word, he would never be on it again.

Over the years I politely greeted the women who followed Dominique as they entered and exited his life. Most of them weren't very kind to him or appreciative, which I didn't understand at the time. I forgive them now entirely for their misbehavior. He made it all too clear they'd never get what they wanted. He was determined not to give it to them, even as he smothered their objections with his solicitude and generosity, tending dutifully to their frowns and dark moods with cheery inquiries into whether there was anything he could do to make them happier, *darling?*

I don't think he came clean with any of them. He was quick and light on his feet, but it was exhausting for him. It was exhausting for me just to watch. Was it worth it?

"It's hell having dinner alone." He told me that more than once without a trace of humor.

That's why Esther was pissed off with him. In their wild younger days, they had some pact of understanding that gave her certain rights in her brother's life. Then he booked on her, bought a first-class ticket paid for in cash, grabbed a phony passport, and took off for parts unknown, leaving Esther stranded in an arid reality. At least she didn't blame me. Maybe she thought I was a hapless bystander kidnapped by her brother.

Susan knew I'd booked, too. She knew I never really came back from Mexico. She thought it was because I didn't love her. That wasn't true at all. I just couldn't manage to convince her of the totality of my attention to her predicament. Neither Old Leonard nor I, despite our considerable skills of dissimulation, could ever really pull that one off.

seven

THE FUTURE

I DROVE INTO TOWN from Malibu and parked Suzanne's classic red Mercedes coupe—I'd had the engine completely rebuilt—in front of Tremaine. The pizza-oven, midsummer LA heat gave me weird shivers as I stepped out of the car. It was July 1988.

Leonard greeted me at the door. "Come on in, bro. Good to see you upright."

He hadn't installed air conditioning in the apartment yet. The place seemed even more unlived in since my family had moved out. It was twilight-dark inside, the shades drawn to block out the blinding light. He was in his underwear, not the wizened elf yet, a guy still in his prime but exhausted. I'd roused him from his favorite landing pad,

the couch in the living room where he seized any opportunity to collapse.

"I've been shopping for a new car," I announced. The
week before, summoned by the local police, I'd walked up
the hill from our house to find Susan holding infant Sara
in her arms with five-year-old Sam quietly beside her, standing next to the wreck of our Oldsmobile Cutlass she'd
somehow driven off the empty country road, totaling it.
"On the advice of an old friend who is an expert in these
matters, I visited three dealerships to get the best deal."

Leonard shuddered, eyes raised to the heavens. He
quickly ushered me to my corner chair in the kitchen as if
I'd shown up at a hospital ER hemorrhaging. "I'm amazed
you were able to leave your house," he muttered.

"Quite amazing," I muttered back.

"Did you get the new car?"

I shook my head.

"Of course not."

∼

Susan and I weren't picture-takers. Most of our family pho-
tos were taken by others who gave us prints. I have one
from early 1988, a few months before that hot afternoon.
We're outside on the patio in the backyard in Malibu.
Sara is less than six months old. She looks really small on
Susan's lap. I'm sitting in a chair opposite them. Leonard

and my dad are behind us. My mother isn't in the picture. She must be the one who took it.

Leonard was quite fond of my dad, recognizing him as a sympathizer to our cause, a fellow reluctant recruit in the army of the conventional, half in, half out, but not terribly motivated to act out his fantasy of running away to the New Hebrides where, he claimed, he owned property on the island of Espiritu Santo. He told this to everyone he met, embellishing the story with convincing details, including a newspaper clipping he carried in his wallet reporting on the construction of a new power plant *on my island.* A surprising number of people believed him. Leonard didn't, but perfectly understood my father's impulse to fabricate.

Leonard, who never took a bad photo, muscled up for the occasion and poses manfully in his black T-shirt and silver-buckled belt, but you can see—at least I can—what an effort it's taking for him to smile for the camera.

I rarely take a good picture, but I look great in this one, all smiles. I honestly have no idea where my mind was, because only a few weeks, if not days, later, I would stumble—I thought at first it was the flu—then go down completely.

~

"I can't write," I confided to him hoarsely.

"That's the worst." He was definitive. "At least no one else can write either, y'know?" It was a halfhearted attempt at humor. The ongoing strike of the Writers Guild of America against the studios was in its fourth month. The strike committee called me with my picketing assignments, but I was able to beg off, not because of the state of my mind, but my body. I was in as much pain as before the surgery. Despite the surgeon's cheerful prediction that I'd be fine, the two nerves that go all the way down my left leg were permanently damaged. My hip, knee, and ankle didn't work very well, painful even to the touch. My calf was partially numb, and one of my quads lay uselessly on my thigh. As my body struggled to compensate, the spinal pain in my chest and neck became as bad as my leg. Anyway, that's my tale of woe.

Not long after my surgery, Leonard had finally played his new album, *I'm Your Man*, for the Sony execs. This time there was no drama or cryptic pronouncement about the great and the good. The album was handed directly to Sony International without any promotion or tour in America, where it would barely be noticed for many years.

Nice seeing you again, Leonard. Always a pleasure doing business with you.

Despite his best efforts, Leonard had allowed his suckered hopes to lift his toes off the ground, and he came crashing back to earth in a crumpled heap.

"Are you writing?" I asked, as if a distant miracle might cheer me up.

"Maybe I get a line down in the morning. A full day's work."

We thoughtfully munched on some pickles he found in the fridge.

"I'm not sure what's going on," I finally ventured.

"You're wrecked, man," Dr. Cohen pronounced without hesitation, specialist of specialists, the only one who could diagnosis my ailment without even a stethoscope. *You're wrecked, man* became a technical term in our permanent vocabulary.

I detected as well a slight note of celebration in his diagnosis: *Welcome to the club.* It's not as if Leonard wished me ill, but even though we'd been friends for a decade by then, compadres in matters of Roshi and show biz and fatherhood, I'd been oblivious to his fundamental condition as he soldiered on, barely managing a wan smile. How could I have known? He never tried to explain it to me. He'd tried unsuccessfully with other, well-meaning friends, who proved smug in the way well-meaning friends can be.

Oh come on, Leonard, it's not that bad. Cheer up. All you need is a good woman.

"All I need is a good woman," he'd sometimes mutter, barking a laugh as if something was caught in his throat.

He didn't try to explain it to me lest I also recommend a good woman. Instead, he waited patiently for me to join him in his scavenged cardboard box in the homeless part of time.

"I'm surprised you lasted this long." His back was to me as he checked whether there was anything else to eat hiding in the near-empty refrigerator.

"You know how it is," I replied breezily, not at all sure how it is.

"Ohhhh, I surely do know how it is," he stated with conviction. "Like the back of my hand." He put some cheese and crackers on the table like paperweights. He sat down in his chair but turned sideways so we were parallel and could stare together over the counter at the glass-fronted kitchen cabinets reflecting our contemplative faces.

We spent so much time in our formal conversations, but found the greatest comfort in wordless occupation of a shared, enveloping state of mind, even in the darkest dark. We took great care of each other, like simians picking and discarding each other's nits. We weren't always wrecked, although Leonard was of the opinion, which I later came to share, that once you've been truly and thoroughly wrecked—*shattered* was his word—you never fully recover, no matter how much glue and Scotch tape and chewing gum you apply to hold the pieces in place.

This is what it feels like.

This is IT.

Not everything. Not the whole cosmos Roshi encourages us to experience.

Not even the truth.

Mood.

The only reality.

∾

We examined magisterial poetic depictions of depression, from the nineteenth-century *The Anatomy of Melancholy* to F. Scott Fitzgerald's *The Crack-Up* and William Styron's seductive memoir, *Darkness Visible*. We had no interest in joining that club.

Leonard tried meds off and on. I tried meds. I lucked upon one of the most wonderful, compassionate, funny men of medicine I've ever known, a highly respected UCLA psychopharmacologist in the early days of the specialty. On my recommendation Leonard checked him out and became quite fond of him. None of his meds ever worked for me, though, and only variations of prescription amphetamine ever made Leonard feel any better. Then again modest doses of speed always made him feel better.

He may have tried some talk therapy in the past. I'm not sure. For a time I engaged in a comforting dialogue with a brilliant woman, a psychotherapist whose tragic view of life seemed to align with my own.

"It's called cognitive therapy," I informed Leonard.

"I think I've heard of that somewhere."

"The idea seems to be that in this condition you want to avoid undertaking tasks beyond your diminished capacities, since you're bound to fail, which only amplifies your misery."

"Like driving up the dreaded San Vicente."

"Precisely."

The dreaded San Vicente was our shorthand for impossible undertakings of any kind. San Vicente Boulevard contradicted the grid of parallel and perpendicular north/south and east/west thoroughfares of the city, running instead at a forty-five-degree angle, producing a series of challenging intersections that created in certain conditions, such as Leonard's for about twenty-five years, the sensation of driving blindfolded, hair-raising as well for me in the passenger seat beside him.

"At any rate," I went on. "She prescribed a writing regime for me. Every morning I set a timer for five minutes. That's my workday. I stop before my mind overheats dangerously from the internal friction of the enterprise."

"Five minutes? That's terrific!"

I hesitantly agreed.

"But you don't stop?"

"Of course not," I confessed.

"Who could? Do you tell her you can't stop?"

"She's very understanding."

As we pondered this unexpected kindness, an explosion of revving engines shattered the silence. Jack the

Joshu Sasaki Roshi was seventy when I first met him and Leonard at a Zen sesshin in 1977. *(From the collection of Eric Lerner)*

We purchased the duplex in Los Angeles in 1979 mostly for its proximity to Roshi's Zen Center. We would always refer to it by the name of the street: Tremaine. *(From the collection of Eric Lerner)*

The antique pine table, distressed like us, tucked into the little nook in the kitchen in the top-floor apartment, where so much took place. *(From the collection of Eric Lerner)*

In general, Leonard's interest in food was perfunctory. He sometimes sighed: *I wouldn't eat, you know, if it weren't absolutely necessary.* (*Photo by Robert Faggen*)

With our old pal Richard, who sent me to Roshi in the first place.
(From the collection of Eric Lerner)

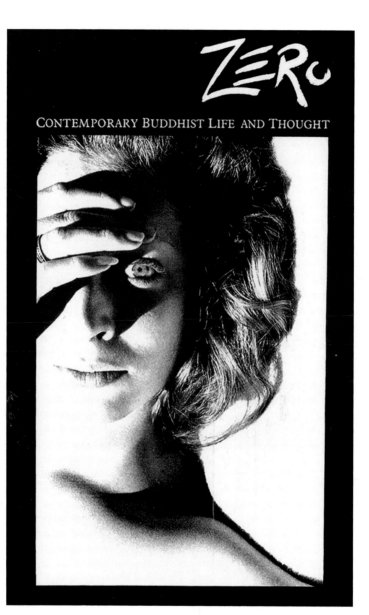

The cover of the first issue, our early joint
enterprise in trying to explicate the vital
matter: What the fuck is Roshi all about?

I went to work in Hollywood in 1983. Leonard provided the young warrior with his battle chariot. *(From the collection of Eric Lerner)*

Leonard playing with my son Sam in our tiny backyard at
Tremaine, 1985. *(From the collection of Eric Lerner)*

Leonard was quite fond of my dad, recognizing him as a sympathizer to our cause, a fellow reluctant recruit in the army of the conventional. In the backyard of the Malibu house, 1988.
(From the collection of Eric Lerner)

Once again in 1993 he got his hopes up for *The Future*.
He had beautiful leather jackets made for the band and
crew and sent four of them to the Lerners, including a
tiny one for then five-year-old Sara.

(Selfie photo by Sara Lerner in my jacket many years later)

In the spring of 1995 I drove out to the Ithaca Zen Center, built by one of Roshi's senior monks, David Radin, and his wife, Marcia.

(From the collection of Eric Lerner)

We shopped for hats from time to time, here with Kezban, his assistant, a lovely woman with a musical accent from her native land of Turkey. *(From the collection of Eric Lerner)*

(*Above*) At 106, Roshi didn't look that much older than the first time I met him, his skin still baby smooth, his eyebrows still dark and alive. It was ridiculous. He bore a remarkable resemblance to the scowling, wild-eyed Zen patriarch, Bodhidharma, in the painting on the wall.
(*From the collection of Eric Lerner*)

(*Right*) Leonard thought it was a catchy title. He was an integral part of making the movie.

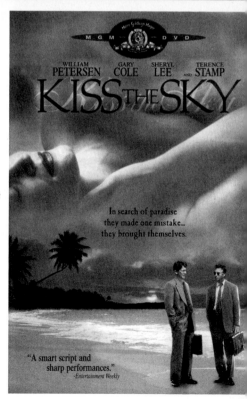

WILLIAM **PETERSEN** GARY **COLE** SHERYL **LEE** AND TERENCE **STAMP**

KISS THE SKY

In search of paradise they made one mistake... they brought themselves.

"A smart script and sharp performances."
-*Entertainment Weekly*

Three Old Boys. *(From the collection of Eric Lerner)*

With Dominique Issermann in New York City, 2014. *(Photo by Eric Lerner)*

"I almost called last night to tell you to put it off."

"I'm glad you didn't."

"Yeah. Me, too."

We watched the cab from the airport pull away.

Our last visit, September 2015.

(Photo by Eric Lerner)

"The writer is ambivalent by nature. That's who we are, Old Eric," he declared. "Our interest in things was never real or whole-hearted. We were mostly interested in life as material for the line, the verse, the story." *(Photo by Eric Lerner)*

old Japanese gardener was attacking the lawn with heavy machinery.

"At least she doesn't insist you try to improve yourself!" Leonard shouted.

"I couldn't bear it if she did!" I shouted back.

~

Despite the enormous popularity of the endeavor, we were too fond of ourselves to believe, much less engage, in self-improvement. Besides, Roshi never suggested that any such improvement was part of the program. For better or worse, we possessed a deep affection—I think it's called amour propre—for our peculiar, particular selves. It was a veritable concrete barrier to personal growth.

Even though we entered the world wrecked, in dire need of a second birth to correct the first one that made us ripe candidates for an extreme spiritual solution, we simply could not embrace the notion that there was anything wrong with us. I can't recall either one of us ever uttering those pathetic words: *I'm so fucked up!*

If we entertained any hopes at all, which we did from time to time, we pinned them on certain circumstances falling in our favor.

A hit changes everything.

~

It's July 16, 1993. Leonard gave a concert that night at the Berklee Performance Center in Boston, part of "The Future Tour" to promote his new album of the same name. The tour had more style and energy and commercial intent than anything he'd done before. He had a snazzy logo for the enterprise—hummingbirds and handcuffs designed by a dear friend of his, Dianne Lawrence. The logo was embroidered on the back of soft, black leather jackets worn by the band and crew. He sent four of them in appropriate sizes to the Lerner family, including a tiny one for five-year-old Sara.

Leonard had pulled himself up off the mat after the knockdown by Sony in the *I'm Your Man* bout, taken a standing eight-count until his head cleared, and come out swinging with another brilliant, even more commercially compelling album.

"Oh man, there's no way Sony can ignore this one!" I fearlessly predicted.

Leonard moistened his lips thoughtfully at my bullish assessment.

While he was squeezing out the lyrics, tunes, and production of his new album in tiny drops of sweat and blood, I had decided—a decision Susan applauded—to quit Hollywood, sell the house in Malibu, and move back to Western Massachusetts. I even found an industrial film company in Boston willing to pay me modest sums to eschew tall tales and write scripts about heavy machinery.

Then unexpectedly the stars realigned. Mel Gibson, at the top of his career, the Sexiest Man Alive, signed on to star in *Bird on a Wire*. I got paid a lot of money. Even better, studio doors opened wide for me to enter and pitch ideas to smiling senior vice presidents who weren't even listening, except to the punch line: *It's like* Bird on a Wire, *y'know?*

We left LA anyway. Susan's Malibu house had zoomed in value in the run-up to the Savings and Loan Scandal, as it was called at the time, which we beat by a month in June 1989. We bought a lovely Victorian house on a tree-lined street near Smith College in Northampton. The kids could walk to school, and I could work on the two script deals I already had in my pocket with the expectation of more to come. A year later *Bird on a Wire* opened and became one of the top ten grossing movies of 1990.

On its way to the screen, though, the studio hired a hack to rewrite the indie, noirish original script into something appropriate for Goldie Hawn, cast opposite Mel Gibson to give the movie four stunning blue eyes. The finished product was marketed as a "romantic-action-comedy," if I've got my genres right. While most of the scenes were inspired by the originals, they appeared on the screen like distortions in the fun-house mirrors of an amusement park, though not amusing to me, even less so because many other people were amused, but in the wrong way. I tried way too many times to explain what I'd actually written: *See, in that first scene where they meet after twenty years . . .*

Oh please. No one was interested.

~

I lived in Cambridge in the late sixties and early seventies, but I'd never even heard of the Berklee Performance Center in Boston until Leonard's show. I arrived two hours before the concert. Susan would join me later, along with my sisters and their husbands and some friends of mine. I was eager for them to see for themselves that Leonard Cohen was still alive.

He couldn't help it. Once again his hopes were running high at the beginning of the tour in Europe. Reviews of the album pulsed with excitement. Sony even booked dates in North America. Most of them were in Canada, though, and the venues in the US were "showcases" like the Berklee Performance Center, small theaters with cachet if you were an aspiring art act.

I walked into the lobby and my heart sank. The theater has since been renovated, but at the time it was a dump. Worse was its modest size, only a thousand seats in a narrow hall. I practically counted them as I walked down the center aisle toward the stage where the crew was making last-minute equipment tweaks. Backstage, Bill Ginn, Leonard's sweet, slightly mad keyboard player who'd sometimes stayed upstairs at Tremaine in the early years, grabbed my hand and whispered, "Really good you showed up early, Eric. We need a night off."

I wasn't sure what he meant until he ushered me over to where Leonard was sitting at a little table in a far corner off the stage, looking as if he was guarding the stack of wooden wine cases beside him. Château Latour.

"Glad you could make it, bro," he greeted me. We rarely shook hands, much less hugged. Old Leonard was not a hugger. He pointed to the chair opposite him as if we were going to play a serious card game like Go Fish. A full bottle was open on the table. I sat down and he filled our glasses.

"I don't drink alone," he reminded me. I understood Bill Ginn's reference to *a night off*.

"Neither do I," I concurred.

We drank with purpose. As we finished the second bottle he confided, "I'm making a heroic attempt to drink all the profits. At a hundred bucks a bottle, I think I have a shot." He glanced around at his surroundings, raising his chin and eyebrows. The dismal situation required no further commentary.

Sony had shafted him again.

"For some curious reason," he began, pulling the cork from a third bottle, "my bass player is intent on sabotaging my efforts."

Only months before Leonard had been so enthused about his new bass player, a widely respected, very hip musician, but months before there had been a surfeit of enthusiasm to go around. I forget whether the problem was that the bass player played too fast or too slow, but Leonard believed, or purported to, that "he's involved in some conspiracy with my drummer."

From then on Leonard and I referred to various acts of knife-in-the-back treachery as: *He did a [name of the bass player] on me.*

"Good wine, eh?"

"Excellent."

It was tasty stuff, from Pauillac, a bit prim for my taste that had been recently upgraded by all those studio checks, but I understood how its somber style suited the mood. He deftly reached into the wooden Bordeaux coffin that cradled the bottles' body and neck and pulled out another.

"They served Château Latour exclusively on the *Titanic*, you know." He delivered the mordant line in the manner of English nobility, nostrils flared, eyes gazing over the horizon, the Lord of All Manners.

Striking poses was extremely important to us, if only to reassure others that we could still stand upright and make funny faces no matter the circumstances. This, though, was a total disaster. Leonard wouldn't go on tour again for fifteen years, and then only because he was so broke he forced himself to overcome the dismal memory of this tour.

"We need a few drops more." Leonard motioned with his empty glass to the wooden case. He handed me the corkscrew. "Could you do the honors? You've got more leverage than me."

Mood is everything.

It may have been Leonard's only certainty, a reminder he often repeated lest we forget and go aimlessly astray. It was his greatest contribution to our puzzling endeavor, if not to mankind's perennial quest for spiritual understanding. Mood is everything and everything else is just speculation. Mood is the actuality of existence. *What it feels like in the bone.*

Whether or not the sages, mystics, masters, or even Roshi believed that, we didn't care. We wanted better moods, and the older he got, the less constrained he felt about pursuing a better mood.

I'm just trying to feel two cents better.

Backstage at the Berklee theater that night Leonard wasn't having any luck with it. Curiously, I was actually in a pretty good mood.

In 1993, while most novelists in America secretly (or not) dreamed of their work becoming a hit movie, I was writing a dark, quirky literary novel intended never to appear on any screen. I hoped for a relatively tiny audience of discriminating readers who'd purposely skipped the network television debut of the studio's mashed-up version of *Bird*

on a Wire that drew forty million viewers on a single Saturday night.

I took the phone off the hook in my top-floor office in an old brick Victorian building in downtown Northampton even though it was still ringing with offers from Hollywood. With the practiced, dedicated speed of a screenwriter, it took me only four months to turn out the first half of my novel. I express-mailed it to Leonard back in LA. It was called *Sweet Jane.*

He read it in two days.

"It's got no voice," he pronounced matter-of-factly on the phone, without the customary editorial preface of mealymouthed praise prior to the negative judgment.

I waited for some elaboration. I could almost see him frowning because I hadn't immediately grasped his point.

"It's a screenplay. A pretty good one. But it has no voice."

Oh. Shit.

Leonard read everything I wrote. His critiques were invariably compressed, not unlike Roshi's unerring grunts of approval or disapproval.

It has no voice.

There was no mistaking the unspoken corollary: *It's not a novel.*

I tossed the entire manuscript in the trash.

Then something happened, the way something sometimes happens in sanzen. Only it was Leonard's presence in my mind not Roshi's, resonating like a tuning fork as I relentlessly took dictation from a voice I'd never heard before. Six months later I sent him the finished novel.

"It's good, man. You found the voice." He kind of chuckled. "It's a pretty good one, too. Congratulations. You're off the hook."

That's why I was in a good mood backstage that night at the Berklee theater.

$$\sim$$

"This bottle is much nobler than the others, don't you think?" He thoughtfully contemplated his glass as I refilled it.

"It keeps improving with age."

"Like us."

Reports on exactly how many bottles we consumed before the show that night in Boston would vary, but most of the band agreed we set a new record. Over my shoulder Bill Ginn tried to catch Leonard's attention, pointing to his watch.

Leonard slowly got to his feet. "Wish we had more time, but they tell me I have a show to do."

"Are you good to go?"

"Couldn't be better! Is Little Susan coming?"

"Of course."

"Give her my best. I'd love to see her after, but I've got a bus to catch unless my bass player pushes me off the stage. Can't turn my back for a minute."

"I'll keep an eye on him."

"I'm counting on you. I'm passing through New York after this is finally over."

"I'll come down."

"That would be nice."

"The Mayflower?"

"Where else?" He gave me a salute, buttoned his jacket, and headed for the stage without a hint of a wobble in his stride.

eight

JIKAN

WE LIMPED BACK TO Roshi. Leonard limped first and after a while I limped back, too. We began to describe most of our activities as *limping along*.

Backstage at the concert in Boston in 1993, drinking innumerable bottles of Château Latour, we didn't dismiss the possibility that a hit could change everything, but Leonard was too exhausted and dispirited to continue the chase. *The Future* dimmed from bright and promising to dismally familiar. Leonard wouldn't record another studio album for eight years. After we conducted a thorough postmortem at the Mayflower at the end of the tour, he returned to LA. I didn't hear from him for a couple of weeks despite leaving messages on his answering machine.

Finally, he called. "Ooooooold Eric?"

"Old Boy! I was getting a little worried."

"Not to worry. Everything is wonderful! Guess where I've been?"

We didn't usually ask each other to guess anything.

"Um, Tijuana?"

"Close. Up at Baldy."

"Really?"

"Yup. I did a sesshin."

Neither of us had done a sesshin in years.

"And how was that?"

"Fantastic!" His enthusiasm was slightly alarming. "Roshi's cut out all the bullshit. The guy is amazing. He's *eighty-five* years old and has more energy than his students. The only thing he's interested in now is finding someone who finally gets what he's talking about."

"Interesting." This sudden development made me nervous.

"You still have your old black robes hanging in the closet?" he asked.

"Somewhere."

"Grab 'em and get on a plane. I'm not kidding."

He wasn't kidding. Nevertheless, it felt like he was touting an herbal remedy for my life-threatening condition.

～

One of the biggest agencies in Hollywood had concurred with Leonard's enthusiastic assessment of my novel *Sweet*

Jane. They told me they'd get it published, no problem, after they packaged it as a big movie.

But it's not a big movie! I shouted. *It's a dark, quirky, literary oeuvre. It's my ticket out of Hollywood to higher, hallowed ground.*

Actually, I didn't shout or even mutter any of that. I nodded dumbly, unable to resist the terms of the Faustian bargain they were whispering in my ear—the names of the biggest female stars of the day whom they represented, nubile temptations for any novelist, even this jaded screenwriter.

Six months later, in early 1994, still waiting for *Michelle* to finish reading the manuscript, it was submitted starless to the studios for a quick sale. That same weekend the massive Northridge earthquake paralyzed the entire city for a couple of weeks, an eon in Hollywood time. Digging out of the rubble, we (whoever *we* were by then) barely managed to land a development deal at MGM. I really didn't care. I was glad my novel was finally going to publishers.

"I've never had this happen to me before," the New York agent mused after forwarding me twenty rejection letters from all the major publishing houses. "Each one is for an entirely different reason."

"Apparently no one got it." I could still manage to bite my tongue in those days, rather than scream: *Because you billed my dark literary masterpiece as SMART BEACH FICTION!*

MGM paid me a lot of money to write draft after draft of a screenplay from my manuscript. I was Dr. Frankenstein cutting up his creation and sewing its parts back together grotesquely, until they tossed the monstrosity back to me.

"Not meant to be," Leonard concluded succinctly.

That terminated my brief good mood. It was a mere prelude to the worst time of my life.

The Northridge earthquake seemed to fissure Susan as well, shaking apart what had perhaps been only lightly held in place for a long time. What follows is only a version, the version Leonard and I agreed on. I don't know how much, if any of it, corresponds to Susan's version of what she experienced.

One Sunday afternoon she walked in the door of our house in Northampton, returning from an academic conference—she was working on a master's degree in plant pathology at the time—and it was startlingly apparent that a break had occurred between who she was before—her moods, thoughts, feelings, and perceptions—and who she was now. The gaping fissure had gobbled up the solid ground beneath her feet. Before, despite almost comic differences in our personalities, Susan and I usually concurred about whether something was important or ridiculous, precious or inessential. We thought the same things were funny.

Suddenly nothing was funny. A wall went up between us. The bricks piled higher during the night and the mortar hardened in the morning until we couldn't see or even hear each other on opposite sides of the wall.

It's an episode of clinical depression, Dr. Lerner declared, trying to make sense of it. In those salad days of *Prozac Nation,* hopes ran high for relief from the crushing black mood of the ailment, because, according to the new litany, depression has episodes with beginnings, middles, and ends, and the end could be hastened by new drugs. I rushed Susan from one doc to another, one diagnosis after another, one therapist after another, one med after another. Of course it had something to do with *us.* With *me.* I was simultaneously her caretaker and the cause of her misery. She managed to soldier on as the skillful, loving mother of our kids she'd always been. The family somehow continued to thrive within the confines of our house, even as we became increasingly cut off from the world outside. It went on for nearly a decade.

Leonard called frequently. He kept track of every appointment with a new doctor. "How is the little creature? Any change for the better?"

Leonard and I were rarely somber about anything, but *This is no joke* became the refrain of the dirge we now sang together.

It was suggested to me from various quarters that I leave Susan for my own good, the good of the kids, and even Susan's good.

"I can't leave."

"Of course you can't." Leonard never considered it an option. "We're not one of those guys. We wish we were, but we're not."

Our conversation became more and more exclusionary. I didn't talk about it to anyone else the way we talked about it for ten years.

"I'm worried about you."

"I'm a bit alarmed myself," I conceded.

He knew what I was telling myself: *It will pass. Susan will get better. I can tough it out.*

"What good will it do anyone, especially Susan, if you go down with the ship? You can't operate when you're wrecked. You know that. Your body is shot and your mind is barely attached by a few threads." Leonard was insistent. "Your only hope right now is Roshi." He'd never pressed me this way before.

It was easy for him to say, I thought, because he really was Old Leonard by then. His kids were in their twenties, even if they were still stumbling around, but mine were seven and twelve. It felt like a joke calling myself Old Eric. The only way I knew how to pay the bills was to pitch fairy tales to suits holding other people's checkbooks. I resented Leonard for resurrecting the tattered spiritual battle standard and yelling: *Charge!*

He came to Northampton and stayed with us until I relented.

Thank you, Old Boy.

~

In upstate New York one of Roshi's senior monks and his wife built a rural facility for Roshi with a zendo, a dining hall, another hall for his talks, and an added touch that everyone including Roshi loved, a sauna beside a pond in the woods. In the spring of 1995 I drove out to Ithaca Zen Center.

"It's terrific, eh?" Leonard declared as we sat in the sauna after he'd taken me on a tour of the place. He tossed a bowl of cold water on the glowing stones heated by a wood fire, and the cloud of steam seared our nostrils. He poured another bowl over his head, rubbing his buzz-cut skull with feline pleasure. His appearance was arresting. His thick head of hair had always been one of his most prominent features.

He practically danced naked out of the sauna and plunged into the icy spring water of the pond, shaking himself off like a puppy, then joining me on the top bench of the sauna. The combination of his ascetic look and his giddy mood was unsettling, but I tried to quash my petty suspicions that he couldn't really be *happy*. Aren't you supposed to rejoice in your friend's happiness? Over the years, he'd never been skeptical about my brief moments of elevation, but he was always a more generous spirit than me.

"I once loved cold water," I finally remarked. "But my body isn't too fond of surprises these days."

I couldn't even sit zazen anymore. A decade after my back surgery none of the nerve damage had regenerated. I'm not much for pain-scale numbers. I measure mine in lightning bolts and flashing stars behind closed eyes. I still need to write in a reclining chair with a makeshift keyboard desk across my lap. Standing is a drag and the worst possible posture is sitting with my legs crossed.

"Don't worry about it," Leonard assured me. Old Eric was granted invalid status to sit as best he could even if I had to break out of formal zazen posture or use one of those pansy meditation benches that you kneel on. I had my spot in the zendo beside Leonard, and I showed up when I could.

~

Roshi was concerned about me, too.

"Ahh, Elic, how is your body? Renard tell me."

"Hurts, but okay. Thank you, Roshi. How are you?"

"Ahh, Roshi very old. Hurts, too."

What the hell, we were two hurting Old Guys.

I first encountered him when I was twenty-eight, when everything was so vividly, excruciatingly *real*, the fundamental characteristic of realness at twenty-eight being a dizzying mixture of hope and dread and desire and utter obliviousness to everything except what you want or can't stand. I could barely pay attention to him then, even though I wanted him to empty my mind of what prevented me from paying attention to him.

. I wanted to feel better.

Returning after so many years, I still wanted to feel better but in a weary way that made it so much easier. Before, I'd been peering through some bubble that surrounded me, trying to reach out to touch him through my encasement. He was patient back then, having learned how to deal with children, talking to me in baby talk about Buddha nature and giving me small treats, making clucking sounds of parental approval over my minor accomplishments, the way you display your five-year-old's mediocre drawings on the refrigerator door.

It was different now. I recited my old koan about the guy hanging from the tree branch, but Roshi didn't seem very interested in him. All he was interested in, as Leonard advertised, was true nature.

Meet me where I am.

He embraced me in a cosmic bear hug and whispered in my ear, "Absolute love. That's all there is."

"Really? He said that?"

Leonard wanted daily reports. I had the feeling he and Roshi were consulting regarding my condition. After lunch we'd walk up the path in the woods and hang out smoking cigarettes. I resented Leonard's high spirits less and less each day.

~

"How do you realize your true nature when you look at Susan's face?" Roshi asked me, demonstrating by doing a scary-real mime of human distress. He looked at me kind of sideways and sighed like doctors do before delivering a difficult diagnosis. "Mmm. Maybe you monk."

What?

"Maybe you monk," he repeated. He rang his dismissal bell.

~

"He said something like that last night after a couple of drinks," Leonard cautiously confirmed: *Elic should be monk.*

"Or Elic should be astronaut. Mission to Mars."

Leonard puffed in thoughtful silence. "I'm going to ordain when we get back to LA."

Once again I was unnerved. *Don't leave me!*

"It's not that big a deal," he tried to reassure me. "I get an even shorter haircut and some fancy duds. I'll be fine. But you're not. Roshi said: *Elic in big trouble.*"

Of course I was. "Maybe I could do a couple of sesshins a year."

"Or five or six?" Leonard offered the bait to see if I'd rise to it, knowing perfectly well I have a hard time dismissing even the wackiest new idea.

"I could show up at pitch meetings with a bald head," I joked. "Screenwriters are supposed to look like slovenly children."

"Then you could come up to Baldy and write your scripts."

"Could I?"

"Why not? We'll figure something out."

"Where would I live?"

"Not so important. A monk without portfolio."

"Maybe less of me would do Susan some good."

"*Less is more* has always been my position in these matters."

We were getting excited.

~

In late December 1996 Leonard picked me up at the Ontario, California, airport, an hour's drive from Baldy. We drove up the mountain in his new Nissan Pathfinder, the car he would keep for the rest of his life, the perfect vehicle for the new Old Leonard, the shaven-headed monk Roshi named *Jikan*. I'd never seen Leonard in jeans before. It was a fundamental principle of his style. Now he was wearing Carhartt-type black work jeans along with a shapeless jacket over his long underwear.

"Cold up there," he announced, showing off by whipping his new four-wheel-drive vehicle around the tight turns up the mountain. I was dizzy on memory and anticipation. On my arrival, Roshi's students from my old days embraced me, some of them monks now. It was Rohatsu, the once-a-year slugfest of extreme practice that had been my initiation to Baldy almost twenty years ago.

Leonard had moved up to Baldy the year before.

"I'm done, man."

He was in the process of selling his writer's catalog of songs to Sony. The considerable proceeds would give him enough money to live on and take care of his kids and their mother for the duration without his having to make another album again. "I gotta tell you, not needing a hit to change everything *really* changes everything."

The deliberately harsh physical conditions up at Baldy were integral to the regimen. At sixty, though, Leonard knew he couldn't endure the cold, the sleep deprivation, and the outdoor plumbing for very long. Moreover, residents at Mt. Baldy devote themselves full-time to their study with Roshi. If you weren't in the zendo, you were working as a cook, administrator, maintenance person, or Roshi's attendant. You had almost no time to yourself.

Roshi and Leonard, however, came up with a special arrangement. Leonard had always been special to Roshi. Leonard would always be Roshi's student, but they easily slipped in and out of being boyz. Leonard explained to me that instead of fixing roofs or cutting up vegetables in the kitchen, he would work on his poetry or drawings or whatever he wanted to do now that he was finally free from the brutal alchemy of transmuting creation into bucks.

"He gets it," Leonard declared, a fervent prayer of thanks.

There was a ramshackle arts-and-crafts cabin, unused since the Boy Scout camp days, that Roshi gave to Leonard. He'd always been an accomplished funky-house remodeler, first the house high up the winding steps on the Greek island of Hydra in the early sixties, then his place in Montreal, and even his apartment at Tremaine. He outdid himself with his little Baldy cabin, dividing the small space into a bedroom and workroom less than ten feet by ten that neatly accommodated a desk, keyboard, amp, recording devices, and even a tiny kitchen with a coffee station, hot plate, and fridge. He shored up the foundation, insulated the walls, replaced the roof, and installed a heater, electricity, and a phone line. He equipped the cabin with indoor plumbing, building a small bathroom with shower and toilet, amenities no one else at Baldy had except Roshi.

He gave the phone number to no one except his kids and manager, not even me. I would leave a message on the answering machine at Tremaine and he'd call me back unless he was in the middle of a sesshin.

"Not bad, eh?" Leonard bragged as he showed off every detail of his compact new home. For the sesshin he'd commandeered another bed for me and squeezed it into the front room of his cabin.

"I hope you like instant coffee. I've grown quite fond of it with evaporated milk. I may never go back to the real thing. I get up extra early for a cup at two thirty. Glad you could make it, bro."

Me, too. We had the most fun we ever had together that week.

Remember that time up at Baldy?

~

I couldn't sit in the zendo without disturbing the near maniacal formality of Baldy, so I did my zazen in the "second zendo," the small meditation hall across from the main zendo. Each night Leonard and I trudged in silence back to the cabin after the final late-night sanzen and climbed the steep steps to his cabin. Closing the door behind us we burst into furtive reports on the day's events, maintaining our high standards of poetics.

"I walked out of sanzen today and I thought: *Careful, Old Leonard, 'cause you really are old and while it wouldn't be the worst way to go—stumbling on this steep, icy path on your way back to the zendo—it's kind of nice being alive right now because everything is on fire.*"

We never made specific claims, just the facts.

"What sort of fire?"

"Like acid, but much better because I was part of the conflagration."

"How long did it last?"

"I tried to make it last as long as I could. I practically tiptoed back to the zendo."

"Any idea why it all went up in flames?"

"Roshi was particularly brilliant in sanzen."

"Or you were."

"You're too kind."

~

"It's perfect up here," he mused one night. "I don't have to talk to anyone except Roshi. I say hi and good-bye and exchange a few words with the other monks. They're nice kids. Roshi put out the word: *Leave Renard alone.* What can I say? I just can't stand people anymore."

He smiled a crooked grin, as if: *Ha, I finally said it!* He had claimed the reclusiveness that would define the rest of his life, perfecting his solitary state with the same attention to detail and craftsmanship he applied to all his work. He developed a precise calculus of what he wanted to do, what he ought to do, and what he could not skip out of doing.

There were his kids. There was that other thing: *It's hell to have dinner alone.* There would always be business to attend to. Otherwise, he hoarded his time. He had no regrets. He was content to be a recluse, balancing as best he could loneliness with his beloved solitude that he cultivated like a garden. Years later I finally joined him in that garden where he'd been patiently tending his patch, waiting for me.

~

"I stopped doing zazen," I reported on the fourth evening.

He was alarmed. "You stopped doing the sesshin?"

"No. I'm still doing it."

I explained how I'd been doing zazen up in the second zendo for the first few days as best I could with my wrecked spine. I would listen for the bells from the main zendo that commenced and ended each zazen period, and I'd go outside to join the snaking line marching around in lockstep. I went with everyone else to sanzen and meals and chanting and teisho. But I stopped doing zazen.

"I was getting bored."

"I find it incredibly boring sometimes."

"Don't worry," I reassured him. He thought I might pack my bag and leave. "Sanzen is fine. I just stopped doing zazen."

"You told Roshi?"

"I didn't have to. I showed up and my eyes weren't crossed and my head wasn't exploding. I did the bows and, um, there we were."

"No shit?"

"No shit."

"That's very interesting."

~

Hai, koan.

I'm not sure I even had a koan anymore. I would mumble something and he'd nod or shrug or wave his hand as if: *Let's see, what should we try now?*

Roshi closed his eyes and sang a tuning note. "Ahhhh-hhhhhhhhhh." He opened his eyes, indicating that it was my turn.

"Ahhhhhhhhhhhhhhhh." I ran out of breath.

He considered my performance, then offered a suggestion. "More. Whole body."

He demonstrated with greater gusto. "Ahhhhhhhhhhh hhhhAH!"

I was impressed. He motioned for me to join him in a duet.

"AHHHHHHHHHH."

We stopped and looked at each other.

"Bettah."

I returned to my little empty zendo. I can't recall what I did while everyone else was exerting every ounce of their will and energy to maintain the demanding posture and focus of zazen.

From a certain point of view, I was fucking off.

~

Roshi picked up his little staff made of beautiful polished wood with a curved head, an object of endless fascination on the low table beside him near his bell. He held the staff up and admired it, then urged me to admire it with him.

More. More. Whole body. Whole cosmos.

Elic, Roshi. Same same.

Mind, body. Same same.

Absolute Self, Limited Self. Same same.

~

Every religion has a Founder Story. For the Jews it's Moses and the Red Sea and the Ten Commandments. Christianity recounts how the Founder was nailed up on a cross wondering why God had forsaken him. Then he returns from the dead.

Buddhism, no matter the sect or form it takes, also has a Founder story. There's a guy, not just any guy but a prince, who runs out on his family, his responsibilities, his place in society. He's like the guy Leonard and I often referred to, a mythical figure, the guy who tells the wife he's going out for a pack of cigarettes one day and never comes back.

But there's a difference between the two guys, at least to the Buddhists. They say that while the guy who goes out for cigarettes and the guy who became Buddha *may* have split for the same reason—they couldn't stand it anymore—each left by an entirely different path. The guy who went for cigarettes probably picked up a pint of Ripple at the store as well, a few lottery tickets, maybe had a mistress stashed somewhere. His splitting is unforgivable, totally selfish, and he's going straight to hell.

Buddha, however, hightailed it down a much higher road, the spiritual path to the Bodhi Tree under which he sat, dedicated, chaste, single-minded in his pursuit of enlightenment, not just for himself but for the benefit of all sentient beings, which makes his abandonment of his weeping wife on the doorstep with their small children in her arms okay. Even exemplary.

For twenty-five hundred years Buddha's renunciation inspired enlightenment seekers to don robes, take new names, and quit the world. Leonard quite liked being a monk. Oh sure, he tried to make light of it in the interviews he gave while he was up at Baldy, a pose within a pose, as if no one should take his black dress and Japanese name too seriously: *I would have become Roshi's student of accounting if he'd been an accountant.*

In fact, he always liked uniforms and military rigor, but more importantly, up at Baldy he was off the hook, just like Buddha and Buddhist monks for millennia—out for a pack of cigarettes and gone, but respected for it. What a great deal!

Too bad I couldn't do it.

I'd tried to pull it off before. I went to India in 1973. I arrived at Baldy without a return ticket in 1978. This time I tiptoed even farther out toward the edge of the illusory cliff before I backed away. As I had each time before, I immediately started writing about it.

~

There are these two middle-aged guys, see, but guess who they really are?

I'd never begin a real pitch that way, but I'm pitching something else here. These two guys, see, are actually one mind split in two, portrayed as best friends, but opposites, in constant push and pull, adding up to the sum total of my own disjointed self.

They're stuck in a rut. They can't take it anymore. They tell their wives they're going on some kind of business trip to Indonesia of all places. It's a jailbreak. They land in Jakarta and head straight for a high-class club they've heard about, where they have morose paid sexual encounters and get even more depressed. Then they stumble into an opium den and hear an urgent whisper: *Go to Lake Toba, the highest lake in the world, so high you can look up and Kiss the Sky.*

That's what the movie's called.

Leonard thought it was a catchy title. He was an integral part of making the movie, along with our old pal Richard Cohen (no relation). Richard was the one who'd sent me to Roshi in the first place. He was part of *Zero* as well as the purchase of Tremaine. Then he went to business school and became president of home entertainment at Walt Disney Studios. Richard led a strange life. He opened the video vaults for the first time and made a lot of stockholders rich. In 1997 he was running home entertainment at MGM. A fellow executive in charge of pay TV wanted to make edgy art films for cable. Richard knew just the guy.

∽

Art imitates Life.

Our two fictional heroes, along with our real hero, Eric, head off to the Philippines where there is a viable film industry—we hired the same crew that shot *Apocalypse Now*—and an impressive stand-in for the highest lake in the world. We ascended the slope of a semi-dormant volcano on mules and peered down at an aquamarine lake in the crater below as a chopper zoomed overhead for the establishing shot.

In the story—still keeping fact and fiction distinct—our heroes arrive at a funky guesthouse beside the highest lake in the world, and they get even higher when The Girl shows up. They both fall for her. She's a free spirit who brings along her old pal, a Zen monk named Kozen, pretty much Leonard, played by Terence Stamp, a longtime student of the Indian teacher Krishnamurti.

Bathed in sensual and spiritual delights, spouting dialogue that twists the mind and sensibilities, our heroes decide: *Fuck it, we ain't going home. We found paradise and we're staying.*

Only we'll make it better!

They decide to build, not a tropical resort hotel, but an off-the-grid way station for misfits like themselves beside the highest lake in the world, where you can look up and kiss the sky.

Meanwhile, I was in my own paradise. I had MGM's five-million-dollar budget, distribution on cable, and plans for an art-house release. Best of all, I wasn't just the writer; I'd wrangled my way into being the producer, overseeing the choice of director and cast. The icing on the cake was Leonard's promise of his songs for the soundtrack, practically for free because this was Old Eric's greatest effort ever to publicly answer our most pressing question: *What the fuck is Roshi all about?*

~

During the year of preproduction I commuted from Northampton to LA with my black robes in my traveling bag. At every possible opportunity I raced up the mountain where Leonard had the guest cabin waiting for me.

Roshi liked to entertain in his private hut. I'm not sure what else to call the tiny space connected by a little tunnel to his cabin. Leonard and I crawled inside after evening zendo to hang out on tatami mats with Roshi, who insisted on playing the attentive host, deftly reaching over his shoulder into shelves of pigeonholes crammed with glasses, bottles, chopsticks, bowls, and incense.

One evening his female attendant, his *inji,* the latest in a long line of female attendants stretching back before my time, appeared with plates of fish and rice.

"It's very good," I complimented her. Roshi shrugged and muttered something. The inji slunk off, miffed.

Apparently, Roshi thought the fish was overcooked.

"He's a hard man to please," Leonard whispered to me. Roshi looked at Leonard questioningly. "I tell Eric, Roshi, you are connoisseur. Mmm. *Great expert.*"

Roshi shrugged. *What did you expect?* He picked up the half-empty bottle of sake and admired it, more than the pine tree, as if a lifetime of memories were trapped in the bottle. He considered his glass and made a sad face.

"Cannot drink so much now. Doctor say." He sighed poignantly.

"Sorry to hear it, Roshi."

"You drink, Elic." He filled my empty glass once more.

Another evening the inji brought us bowls of hot noodle soup.

"Like this." Roshi motioned for me to pay attention, not to his manifestation of true self, but to his demonstration of how to eat steamy ramen, by lifting the noodles out of the bowl with your chopsticks high enough to slurp the hanging threads, making noise to indicate you're inhaling cooling air along with the dangerously hot noodles.

The Zen of Noodle Slurping?

Hardly.

At the beginning of my spiritual career in 1969, Zen was at its peak of popularity in America via the writings of D. T. Suzuki and Alan Watts, whose *Zen Flesh Zen Bones* recounted paradoxical tales of ignorant students and wise masters, tales that brought knowing smiles to readers' faces. Since then, the knowing smiles have ripened into a conceit that declares a spare white restaurant, a garden with rocks asymmetrically placed around a pool of water, or a particularly clever use of an emoji to be *Zen-like*. A tech executive with a slim silhouette or a basketball coach who answers a question with a question is a *Zen master*. And haven't we all had a *Zen moment?*

I haven't. Neither did Leonard. I don't think Roshi ever did either.

We were just having a good time in his hut.

Leonard often quoted George Burns, the cigar-smoking comedian who lived to nearly a hundred: *Faking it is the key to life, and if you can fake sincerity, you've got it made.* Roshi had it made. If he was faking sincerity, he had me utterly convinced.

"He likes you because you don't want anything from him. You don't need him to do anything for you," Leonard told me as we stumbled out of the hut back up the long, dark path. After every visit I rewrote parts of the script.

~

Art and Life become confused.

We started shooting on soundstages and in strip clubs in Manila. For almost two months I lived in a penthouse suite in the Mandarin Oriental Hotel. Each morning I opened my email to find Leonard's latest communication containing a verse whose tagline was always: *A thousand kisses deep.*

Dozens of verses, one each day, some so stunning I emailed back: *Stop! That's the one!*

I didn't ask what he was doing. It wasn't a reflective period in our lives. He was supposed to be the monk Jikan, setting down words in his cabin strictly for his personal enjoyment.

I'm done!

Then why did I hear the melody straining to accompany the lines that were unquestionably lyrics?

Life imitates Art.

The scene is set in a little Italian restaurant in Santa Monica around the corner from one of LA's last art-house movie theaters. That night MGM test-screened the first cut of *Kiss the Sky* for a recruited audience who filled out response cards afterward. The results were quickly tallied and handed over to the MGM execs, including our old pal Richard Cohen, the director, myself, and Jikan the Monk, who'd driven down from Baldy for the screening. We were parsing the information over pasta and red wine, agreeing that the movie was too long, but it was no big deal— directors' cuts are always too long. Otherwise, everyone was encouraged by the response to the screening.

I wasn't as sanguine. "It's not funny," I told Leonard in my hotel room before he drove back up to Baldy. "It's supposed to be funny."

"Well." Leonard paused, as if a thought had ballooned in his mind but he'd let go of the string. "Sometimes it's hard to see the humor in it all."

Over the next six months we cut and recut the movie, screening it twice more. I got my way and it got shorter and funnier. I drove up to Baldy whenever I could, hanging out with Leonard in the kitchen of Roshi's cabin, where he prepared Roshi's meals. He also ran errands for him and was on the phone a lot, making travel arrangements and dealing with administrative details of Roshi's scene. Roshi still had his inji, but she seemed a bit at a loss, popping in and out of the kitchen to ask Leonard what Roshi wanted. The question seemed to preoccupy Leonard.

We still got together some evenings with Roshi, but afterward Leonard didn't walk down the long path with me. Leonard wasn't sleeping in his cabin. He was barely working there either.

"No time," he explained tersely.

It took a few visits before I realized that the sleeping bag in the corner of Roshi's kitchen was his, and that he wasn't joking when he told me, "I sleep in the closet." If he slept at all. He was doing more zazen than anyone else. Unlike the other resident monks, he traveled with Roshi to every sesshin.

Sesshin after sesshin after sesshin.

∿

Art and Life become indistinguishable.

In the penultimate scene of the movie, after the three-way affair with The Girl explodes and she leaves in disgust, our heroes watch helplessly as their last hope for kissing the sky—their half-finished dream hotel—gets blown away in a monster storm that we created in a Philippine forest, using old-fashioned, low-tech special-effects rain towers and a bulldozer to yank the chainsawed legs of our fake hotel until it finally toppled over.

Incredibly, nearly the same scene was replayed six months later back home. We were finishing postproduction, laying Leonard's songs into the soundtrack, about to strike the first print, when lightning struck us first!

MGM went belly-up, a dead whale in the water, closed until further notice and rebooting under new management. *Kiss the Sky* got exactly one showing at an obscure film festival in Florida before disappearing in the maelstrom.

"It was a pretty good little flick," Leonard reminisced. "Not meant to be, I guess."

～

A year later I was sitting in the kitchen upstairs at Tremaine, in town to pitch a new project, staying at his apartment by myself. We'd talked on the phone and he said he was coming down from Baldy that morning, but I also have some memory that it was a complete surprise when he walked in the door dressed in a civilian escapee's outfit. He was shaking slightly as he announced, "I ran away."

"You ran away?"

"I couldn't breathe."

He sat down at the table across from me and took several deep breaths. "I'm not going back up." That was all he'd tell me for a while. "Roshi's pretty angry with me," he said, smiling grimly.

nine

THE WRITER
IS AMBIVALENT

THE ARRIVAL OF THE new millennium was supposed to precipitate a Nostradamus-like technological doomsday called Y2K. Remember? We counted down with mild curiosity. We were just killing time anyway.

I was still praying for rain. That was Leonard's description of my silent incantations for some deus ex machina to dissolve the impermeable membrane that encased Susan and our lives. I continued shuffling back and forth from coast to coast, though I had very little interest in the content of what I was writing beyond the checks for commencement and delivery of drafts.

I stayed with him when I came to town, one thing at least that was familiar in both our lives. He thought he'd made his final move going up to Baldy and becoming a monk: *I'm done, man.* He never anticipated his fall, or leap, off the mountain that landed him back at Tremaine, slightly bewildered, a *where the fuck am I?* look on his face in those days.

He built a recording studio above the guest apartment in the old garage and even installed an outdoor hot tub adjacent to it. I thought it was a bit of a stretch. He liked baths, but Leonard *a hot tub guy?* We were improvising. I respected his attempt to emphasize the recreational aspects of his life by making music into sort of a hobby in between lounging in his hot tub.

See? I'm still done, man.

Sharon Robinson's association with Leonard began in the seventies as his backup singer. She'd since become an accomplished songwriter in her own right. Sharon lived nearby and was delightful company. She began dropping by Tremaine, as did Leanne Ungar, lovely company as well, Leonard's sound engineer on *The Future.* On my visits the four of us had animated conversations over coffee in the morning before I trudged off to meetings and Leonard and the ladies went out to the backyard studio. Leonard resisted calling what they were doing: *working.* He was groping for a new arrangement, not just for the songs but for his life.

"You guys should make an album," I tossed out one morning. Sharon and Leanne's eyes brightened. Leonard frowned. They had nothing to lose, but he did.

He really didn't want to become undone.

～

I once asked him why he rarely sang about women in the third person: *She*. His answer wasn't clear. This song, too, began with him addressing a woman in the second person: *You*. We were at the kitchen table and the ladies had gone home. He was playing me their day's recorded efforts. At the second verse he leaned back, watching me intently as I listened closely to the words of "In My Secret Life," which ends with the title softly chanted over and over.

"What a trip." He might have said it for the first time that evening after he played me the new song. We'd say it to each other over and over in the years to come, but we had no idea then what the years to come would bring, because the feeling we had then was that we had come to the end of some road. Life is full of surprises.

～

Rather than inspiring him to get up for the game one more time, completing the album *Ten New Songs* in 2001 and its quiet public reception gave him a certain confidence to pursue his secular retirement. He began renovating his house in Montreal, where he planned to spend winters gazing out at the snow falling on the park across the street and writing poetry at his dignified leisure.

In 2003 Susan and I split up. The kids were stunned. Even though she and I had become invisible to each other, we hadn't to them. Somehow we'd remained partners as parents, our version of a secret life. I moved out of the house to an apartment in the neighboring mill town, a grim place neither Sam nor Sara wanted to visit. Over that Christmas vacation, the three of us drove up to Montreal to see Leonard. He tended to us like the dazed refugees from a war zone we were, with endless cups of hot tea and smoked-meat sandwiches from the Main. We went out for dinner at Moishes around the corner.

Less than a year later, in the fall of 2004 while I was visiting him again in Montreal, he got a phone call, *the phone call*, warning him to check his investment account. All of his money was gone. A few months later at Tremaine he grimly showed me the muck floating around on the Internet, the worst part of the ordeal, the destruction of his meticulously fortified bunker of privacy. The elegantly reclusive Leonard Cohen was up to his eyeballs in a tawdry rock 'n' roll scandal.

Scrambling to come up with his next mortgage payment and cover his massive legal bills, he hunkered down at Tremaine for several years in constant battle mode, until the legal tide finally turned in his favor. But the money had disappeared. He tried a few monetizing schemes, like selling his drawings in art galleries, before he accepted the unpalatable reality that the only way for him to recover financially was to tour again—the offers were still there for dates in Europe and Canada—something he hadn't remotely wanted to do for the past fifteen years.

"I have no idea how I'm going to get up onstage and sing cold sober. I've never done it before. I'm not sure if I can, much less remember the words to my own songs."

Age had rendered his liver too delicate for the kind of nightly drinking that once fortified him onstage. We put our experienced heads together, inventorying the contents of our medicine cabinets: *Maybe a little of this and a little of that?*

He didn't need much. The thunderous vibration of standing ovations all over the world turned out to be the most elevating, sustaining drug he ever ingested.

～

In February 2012, PEN New England, a chapter of the venerable international organization of writers and literary personages, assembled a committee that included Elvis Costello, Smokey Robinson, Bono, Rosanne Cash, Paul Simon, and Salman Rushdie to select the recipients of its first-ever award celebrating literary excellence in the writing of song lyrics. They chose Chuck Berry and Leonard.

"Wanna come?" Leonard called me a week before the event. "You know how I hate doing these things by myself.

I've been turning down all kinds of awards lately, but I couldn't pass on a chance to meet Chuck Berry. It could be fun. Or not. At least we can have a nice dinner at the hotel."

I was living near Boston then, only a short drive to Copley Plaza where he was staying. A limo waited at the curb outside the stately old hotel to take us to the event. As we walked out he was besieged by a crowd of autograph seekers waving CDs for him to sign. It was the first time I'd experienced his new celebrity with him. He signed a few before we settled into the back of the limo. "Most of them are sent by pros who sell my autograph on eBay," he explained.

Leonard was in the fourth year of his triumph. At the outset in 2008 it was called a "comeback." After the rave reviews in all corners of the press, from *Rolling Stone* to the *New Yorker*, the venues swelled in size. Playing sold-out arenas and stadiums around the world, he ascended to the mythic peak of major stardom.

"I can't even walk out of my hotel to get a hot dog anymore."

"That's rough, Old Boy."

"Oh well, one can get used to anything." He made an exaggerated put-upon face, miming the exasperating travails of fame. In truth, he was quite pleased to have definitively answered in the affirmative the annoying old question: *Leonard Cohen, is he still alive?*

"And to think, Old Eric. I owe it all to her."

Her was his longtime manager and very close friend, virtually a member of his family. Without her Leonard would never have gone back out on tour, a last desperate grasp at a hit that would change everything. Depending on the court document, she had either stolen, borrowed, or taken what she claimed was rightfully hers—all of Leonard's money.

The PEN award ceremony was held at the John F. Kennedy Presidential Library in Boston, overlooking the harbor. In the greenroom beforehand Leonard introduced me to the host of the event, Caroline Kennedy. He also introduced me to Paul Simon and Keith Richards and Chuck Berry and a slew of other musicians who'd shown up for the tribute.

"My friend, Eric."

They probably thought I was his bodyguard in my gray suit and black shirt and tie looming over Old Leonard. I really like musicians and their unpretentiously off-kilter manner when they don't have an instrument in their hands and are happy to make warm small talk.

Salman Rushdie, representing the literary side of this amalgamated gathering, presented Leonard with his award, reading one of his songs as poetry. Ever since his first record, the poems he continued to write were dismissed by the so-called serious poetry establishment because of the scandalous amount of income his songs generated. Leonard came all the way from LA for this award from PEN in part because it was an acknowledgement he'd sought for a long time.

We celebrated that evening in the hotel's Oak Room, demolishing plates of oysters, a lobster or two, and chops, an uncharacteristic feast for the Old Boy that matched his broadly expansive mood.

"I don't know what any of it means," Leonard pronounced thoughtfully. I recognized a preface to a carefully considered topic for examination. "A kind of vindication, I suppose."

Vindication.

It had always been a matter of great importance to us, but until that night it was the goblin whose name could not be uttered even in daylight. For most of our lives we tried— among so many other things we tried—to ameliorate the disturbing ache of our hearts by eliciting from mothers and lovers, teachers and friends, the gods and total strangers, their murmurs, shouts, cries, and hallelujahs of praise and wonder for our mad, manic creations. Instead, the very ones whose admiration and affirmation we most urgently required stared unblinking at us sprawled on our exhaustion couches: *What are you clowns going on about?*

We needed some definitive authority to tell them— not to mention the Yetnikoffs and studio executives, and a whole list of others, a list too long to enumerate—*You got it wrong!*

We needed vindication.

~

I'd given it one more shot a while back. Of course it wouldn't be the last shot, but at the time I told myself it was. I was down as low as I'd ever been in my dark apartment in the old mill town of Easthampton, separated from hearth and home and kids and wife, sustained by take-out pizza eaten standing up staring out the kitchen window. *Oh, Old Eric, you know you're really fucked when you're standing at the kitchen window having dinner. At least find a chair.*

I closed the blinds and wrote another novel in the winter of 2004. This one was about Allan Pinkerton, the legendary nineteenth-century detective, and the woman he hired as the first female detective. It's a tragic love story, but better than that—at least in Leonard's opinion—was Pinkerton's utterly mad ranting narration. Paralyzed by a stroke that renders his memory unreliable, Pinkerton struggles to solve the most important case of his life: *How did she die?*

"It's fucking brilliant, man. I mean it. I couldn't put it down." I'd sent him the first half. "Get back to work. Send me the whole thing as soon as it's finished. Stay in close touch." He couldn't quite restrain himself. "Y'know, you could have skipped most of the story and just had him rant like you do with me on the phone."

The novel made its way into the hands of a legendary "last of the breed" editor, who agreed to publish it if I excised the first seventy-five pages and got Pinkerton out of bed.

Leonard was aghast. I blithely assured him that with my decades of rewriting experience in Hollywood, I could satisfy the editor's shifting, vacillating instructions and still emerge victorious. I was dreaming of vindication. I was dreaming. Six months later I sent Leonard the final proof pages for him to furnish the book with a burbling blurb of praise.

"What the fuck did you DO?" he shouted over the phone.

He'd never been pissed off at me about anything, but he took my reductio ad absurdum personally, the betrayal of an ethic he assumed we shared.

He was right of course: *What the fuck DID I do?*

The novel appeared without a blurb from Leonard. He offered, if I insisted: *A tale well told,* but I judged it less painful for both of us to do without it. I don't think even a testimonial from him declaring it the greatest thing since sliced bread would have mattered in its final bastardized form. Devoid of any coherent idea how to market it, the publisher characterized it as: *a romp.*

"At least you got a novel published," Leonard offered as consolation. "No small feat these days. You can dine out on it for about five years."

~

"What does it taste like?" I asked near the end of our dinner in the Oak Room.

"It's sweet." He shrugged, as if to make less of it in deference to my yet having tasted it.

Sweet.

Of course. Etymologically, *vindication* comes from the same Latin word as *vengeance.* It would have crimped our friendship if it mattered to me as much as it mattered to him. That could be utter bullshit, too. Of course it mattered to me.

"Listen, man." He wanted to cheer me up. "I of all people know what it's like to have your best efforts go unappreciated. It ain't fun. I don't know why, Old Eric, but the stars won't line up for you in this matter."

"Not meant to be?"

"I've been thinking a lot lately about what's meant to be and what's not meant to be."

It seemed to have something to do with the examination of our limited selves that we'd continued to conduct even after they tore down the Mayflower Hotel. The last few years of battering experiences had produced a kind of dazed detachment in both of us—detached the way a live flame detaches a slug burrowed into your skin—a sense of ourselves as simply the sum of what is meant to be.

"I've never really had what you had, Old Eric," he began. "What you had, and lost, and had again. That real thing with a woman, that psychosexual whatever: *Love.* I only know what you've described to me. And it's taken me a long time to come to terms with the fact that I'm never going to have it."

It was the first time he'd said anything like that to me. I tried it on for size. "So you got the applause and I got the girl?"

"You've still got the girl."

"Very true."

I'd introduced him to Jennifer not long after we met in 2004. Now we were married. "She's not just beautiful and smart and totally gets it, she's nice. She's nice to *you!* I never bumped into the right chick. Or I did and had no idea who she was. I seem to be incapable. Or—*it's just not meant to be.*"

"It's mysterious." I felt better.

"No shit, Sherlock. The only reason I'm in a very good mood is because my once dear friend stole all my money and tried to destroy me."

"It was a close call."

"The whole thing's been a very close call."

$\sim$

Near the end of his last tour he played Boston and invited me and Jennifer to join him for dinner backstage before the show. Roscoe Beck, Leonard's bass player and band-leader, told me in his Texas drawl, "You're the only one Leonard's allowed backstage on the whole tour, except for Carla Bruni in Paris. Not 'cause she's a singer, but 'cause she's the wife of the president of France."

The anecdote is not to brag, but to corroborate Leonard's own description of his life for those five years: *I do the tour like a sesshin.*

Except he was the one ringing the bells and banging the clappers, as well as The Master giving sanzen onstage, overwhelming his audiences with the generosity of his extended performances, returning for curtain calls until the house lights finally came up, then disappearing.

"There's a car waiting outside to take me straight back to my hotel room. They leave me alone all day. I don't show up again until the next afternoon for the sound check, then I go back to my room." He relished the details. "I have a stage to perform on with a band that cooks. The audience applauds. I bow and I leave. Pretty great, huh?"

In the nick of time, when he least expected it, he was finally able to live his life on his own terms. He was off the hook, every hook, the whole rack of hooks. But he remained vigilant, zealously protecting his good mood, eschewing the ancillary rewards of fame and acclaim for his own idiosyncratic idea of treasure: the solitude he found in the welcoming emptiness of his hotel rooms.

~

I really can't stand people anymore.

The stark words on the page lack the melody of his upbeat detachment, without a note of bitterness, not even a flat third of the blues. Nevertheless, like so many things we said to each other, it was both true and not true. It was another of his cover stories.

Whenever I ran into his comrades from the tour—musicians and backup singers I'd known for years, even roadies and foreign tour managers I'd never met before—they always wanted to share their *Old Leonard moments* with me, profound, life-altering encounters. He was a hermit, but the curious truth was that he got great pleasure out of a certain kind of human interaction, giving others pleasure with his attentive company, his empathy, and his magic. He was magic. He liked being magic, as long as he didn't slip and want, much less expect, anything in return.

"The writer is ambivalent by nature. That's who we are," he declared as we finished dinner. It wasn't a change in the topic, but an attempt by Leonard to sum it all up.

I always thought my mother was the most ambivalent person I'd ever known. She freely described herself that way. The last thing I ever considered myself to be was

ambivalent. But Leonard was indicating some other meaning that had nothing to do with *mixed feelings.*

"We're ambivalent about everything, Old Eric. Our
interest in things was never real. It wasn't genuine, or
wholehearted." Leonard spoke in a mournful tone of acceptance. "We were mostly interested in life as material
for the line, the verse, the story. Unfortunately, that didn't
keep us from running around like chickens with our heads
cut off trying to feel a little better, looking for a buzz. Anything to escape the anguish. You know?"

Of course I knew. "We were never *all in.*"

"Not even close."

"We barely had our toes in the water."

"That's why we could never pull off the spiritual solution, go for broke, like those guys freezing their asses off
in the snow outside the monastery, willing to die or kill the
ego or whatever the fuck that's all about. We gave it a shot,
though. Didn't we?"

I shrugged. "Half-assed attempts."

"At best."

"We aren't just twice-born, we're twice-cursed." I saw
it now as clearly as he did. "Writers *and* seekers. Even the
brilliant Dr. James didn't know about that. Or maybe he
did. He was quite interested in mind-altering drugs."

"Our ambivalence pisses them off." Leonard looked a
bit penitent.

"The girls?"

"Yeah."

"We did our best."

"We struck a valiant pose."

We were the last diners in the Oak Room, lingering over good cognac. Chuck Berry stopped by for a bit of banter. Before bidding us good night he invited us to fall by his restaurant in St. Louis if we were ever in the neighborhood.

"I'll bet he's going hunting for pussy," Leonard observed as Chuck walked right past the elevators in the lobby and out the door of the hotel. We finished our drinks and rose from the table. We never made elaborate farewells. Leonard told me to pass his best wishes on to Jennifer, bowed, and walked out of the restaurant, heading for his room upstairs.

Alone.

ten

THE FINISHED PUZZLE FALLS APART

I COULDN'T BREATHE.

That was Leonard's explanation to me for fleeing Roshi in the late nineties. But an even bigger surprise was the phone call I got from him not long after that.

"Guess where I've been?" He didn't give me a chance to guess, he was so pleased with himself. "Mumbai, India."

"You're kidding?"

He'd gone to *study with*—I'm not sure if he called it that, maybe the more innocuous *hang out with*—an Indian teacher, a guru named Ramesh Balsekar.

Leonard explained to me that Balsekar didn't teach meditation or any other spiritual practice. He gave daily talks, *satsang,* which Leonard attended at Ramesh's house, a short walk from the comfy little digs Leonard found for himself in Mumbai. Leonard described Balsekar's scene as a trauma recovery ward for spiritual seekers burnt out on various practices that had done nothing for them, the implication being that he was one of them.

I couldn't breathe.

According to Balsekar, as quoted to me by Leonard, there is nothing to be done in the matter of becoming enlightened, because if it is not part of "your program" to become enlightened you will never become enlightened.

So stop trying.

Leonard followed Balsekar's suggestion and stopped trying. Whatever that meant. I was skeptical. Balsekar's teaching wasn't new to me; it was where I'd started at nineteen. After my first acid trip, I gobbled up translations of the *Upanishads* and the *Bhagavad Gita,* the basic texts of Advaita Vedanta, the ancient lineage of Indian philosophy from which Balsekar descends. I ended up studying Sanskrit at Harvard, hoping to absorb liberation by osmosis, until I decided that changing my mind from the outside in was an exercise in futility. I began the practice purportedly espoused by the Buddha and adopted another conceptual framework called Buddhism.

Then I bumped into Roshi. And Leonard.

From the beginning, he and I agreed that all conceptual frameworks are simply more blah-blah-blah. Now, however,

Leonard had returned from his first pilgrimage to the East with precious souvenirs, a new catechism, albeit an elegant, compelling expression of what might be called *Ultimate Truth*. To me it was just another nice idea.

It made Leonard feel better, though, and naturally he wanted me to feel better. I appreciated his concern. He gave me Balsekar's books to read, and in case I was lagging behind, he read them to me, quoting *Ramesh* before I'd finished my first cup of morning coffee.

"There is doing but there is no doer."

Leonard was firmly convinced that Balsekar's words alone—since all Balsekar did was talk—had hipped him to the truth. The proof was that he could breathe again. Sensing my resistance to this simple equation of cause and effect, he assured me, "He's basically saying the same thing as Roshi."

Except with Roshi we never quoted "the words of the master." One of the best things about Roshi was that you couldn't quote him even if you tried. And Roshi never offered transcendent pearls of wisdom, or even a few catchy phrases to live by.

Leonard wanted me to go with him on his next trip to Mumbai.

"No thanks, man."

~

In early 2005, only a few months after Leonard got *the phone call* and discovered he was broke and in legal hell, I visited him at Tremaine. Following a particularly arduous morning of phone calls with lawyers and accountants Leonard paused, as if checking a thermometer he'd just pulled out of his ass, and announced, "It's amazing, but I really don't feel too bad about all of this."

By then he'd made several trips to India to hang out with Balsekar. I couldn't deny that some fundamental change had taken place. The Old Boy was genuinely in a better mood.

"Oh, I still feel awful about it all," he shrugged, avoiding any new debate over the cause of his better mood and Balsekar's role in it. "But not the anguish. I don't feel that anymore. That's the line of demarcation. Most things annoy me, but they don't, y'know, drag me underwater."

It was true. He wasn't putting it on. I'd seen enough spiritual fairy dust over the years to recognize it. Something had happened to him. But despite the credit he gave Balsekar, first to me and then publicly, it had nothing to do with the Indian guru or his new vocabulary.

Roshi did it to him.

~

Leonard's goals were relatively modest when he limped back to Roshi years before: *I just want to feel two cents better.* His cabin up on Baldy was intended to be, at least in

Leonard's mind, a kind of luxurious retirement home, a gated community with unlimited access, not to an adjacent golf course, but to his master and dear friend, Roshi.

Did Roshi con Leonard into shaving his head and coming up the mountain with his *you can have it all* pitch? Or did Leonard get up there and forget why he came?

Maybe he didn't even realize what was happening, but at some point during all those sesshins—buzz after buzz after buzz—the great transcendental urge to make the buzz permanent rose up in him once more, or maybe for the very first time. Literally or figuratively he threw himself at Roshi's feet.

I want what you got. Lay it on me.

Roshi obliged him and Leonard ended up a hollow-eyed wreck, sleeping in Roshi's closet. That's where Leonard grasped some deep sense of who he was, what he is, how he is, and what he could and couldn't do.

Near the end of 2012, the year of the PEN award ceremony in Boston, Leonard emailed me a link to a blog post on a website I'd never heard of: *Sweeping Zen—The Definitive Online Who's Who in Zen.* Unless it was a sarcastic send-up, it sounded utterly inane to me. The post, "Everybody Knows—Kyozan Joshu Sasaki Roshi and Rinzai-ji," was a snide reference to the title of Leonard's well-known song. It was written by Eshu Martin, who described himself at the time as "the guiding force behind the Victoria Zen Centre in Canada having been ordained as a monk by Sasaki Roshi in 1999, and having practiced in the Rinzai-ji lineage until 2008."

Martin accused Roshi of engaging in sexually inappropriate relationships with his female students for more than fifty years, groping them during sanzen and having affairs with more than a few, some of whom were married. He characterized Roshi's acts as "frequent," "nonconsensual," and "sexually coercive," and he accused the entire Rinzai-ji organization of knowing about Roshi's misdeeds and covering them up for decades.

In the spiritual world of 2012, Zen was far less significant than it had been in decades past, dwarfed in popularity by Insight Meditation and yoga. The blog probably had an audience numbering in the hundreds. Fifty years after Joshu Sasaki Roshi started teaching in America, few outside his small scene had even heard of him. A religious sex scandal is a surefire attention getter, though.

Over the next few months Leonard continued sending me links to the burgeoning brouhaha. Former students came out of the woodwork to take sides. The *New York Times* picked up Eshu Martin's accusations and made them part of a larger story on sexual misconduct in alternative religions in America. The *Los Angeles Times* did a big story on the scandal in the local Zen master's community.

While he was a monk up at Baldy years before, believing that he was done with his career, in an uncharacteristic fit of exuberance Leonard publicly praised Roshi effusively. Now every media story about Roshi invariably cited Leonard's longtime association with the Zen master.

Leonard had to retake control of the narrative, as they say these days. He revised the story of his spiritual life, minimizing Roshi's part in it, crediting Ramesh Balsekar for curing him of his *depression* after he left Mt. Baldy, a word we never used in upper or lowercase to describe our condition.

In his final interview in the *New Yorker*, Leonard characterized Roshi as merely one of his teachers and influences. I laughed when I read it. Brilliant, Old Boy! Wonderful sleight of hand!

For the previous decade, right up to the Old Man's death, Leonard and Roshi were never closer.

∽

I don't think anyone came to Joshu Sasaki Roshi to simply practice meditation, study Zen, or even to participate in a spiritual community. You came for some kind of enlightenment, whatever you imagined that to be. You stayed— that is *if* you stayed—for more complicated reasons.

The transmission of spiritual authority from a roshi to his designated spiritual heir is known as *inka shomei,* "the formal recognition of Zen's deepest realization."

Ostensibly, Joshu Sasaki Roshi came to America in 1962 to establish a new, local lineage that would last far beyond his lifetime. One of the first English words he learned was: *successa.* This was the luscious carrot he dangled in front of his students from the day he arrived.

Early in his teaching career, groups of students in other parts of America, Europe, and even New Zealand invited Roshi to come and give sesshin. If the group became viable enough, Roshi sent one of his senior monks, an osho, to take charge and form an official Rinzai-ji Zen center.

An osho is not a roshi. He or she could not give sanzen. No one bowed or prostrated to them, even though they were expected to attract students and build their centers on their own. It was a tough assignment, far from Mt. Baldy, where everyone expected that one day the equivalent of a plume of white smoke would rise from the sanzen room, a bell would sound, and Roshi would pronounce: *Hai. Successa.*

Years went by. Monks and oshos were ordained. Monks and oshos left, some quietly, some quite pissed off. Years became decades. At the turn of the century Roshi was ninety-three. He got sick, he got well. He cut back his traveling schedule, though he continued to give the three-month training at Baldy. Some oshos had studied with him for most of their adult lives. There was still no successor.

Then Roshi got really sick. Most hundred-year-olds die quickly and peacefully if their bodies are besieged by voracious bacterial infections. It ain't a bad way to go. Leonard sat at his bedside in Cedars-Sinai, the fanciest hospital in Los Angeles. He'd taken charge of Roshi's medical care years before; his own internist became Roshi's doc. Leonard kept me posted on this latest health crisis. It seemed like the end, until they stuck a feeding tube into the dying old man.

"Not my call," he informed me. Roshi was released from the hospital and returned to his quarters at Cimarron Zen Center. He was quite miserable. During breaks in his touring, Leonard visited him almost daily, reporting to me that some days Roshi seemed to be raving, other days he was lucid.

Then the scandal broke.

Now the story catches up with my visit to Tremaine in May 2013 that I recounted earlier, the week Leonard and I conducted our examination of the Neanderthals and the Neo-Sabbatians. The phone rang one morning and as always he let it go to voicemail: *Hello. I can't answer your call right now. Please leave a message.*

Hearing the woman's voice leaving her message, Leonard quickly picked up. It was Roshi's inji. Leonard spoke to her briefly and returned to the kitchen smiling. "She says Roshi's doing better today. He wants me to come by for an early dinner. I'll pick up a bunch of sushi."

"You're kidding. Sushi?"

"That's what he wants if he's feeling decent. He's hard to kill. I asked if you could come over with me. She asked Roshi and he said yes."

We were jazzed by the good news. Leonard told me before I arrived in town that he hoped I would get to see Roshi, even though he was in such poor, unpredictable health, because, Leonard practically whispered to me over the phone, "Sometimes it's like being in sanzen."

Sanzen?

～

It was therefore with a mixture of skepticism and veneration that I accompanied Leonard to pay a sick call to our old master. Kezban, Leonard's assistant of the past few years, drove. She's a lovely woman with a musical accent from her native land of Turkey, with an innocent appreciation of Leonard's eccentricities, including his old friends. That night she bought enough sushi in Styrofoam take-out containers to cater a wedding.

Though I'd spent a lot of time with Roshi up at Baldy in the nineties, I hadn't been back to Cimarron Zen Center in more than thirty years. We parked outside the gate, and I immediately slipped into some mystic-poetic-metaphorical state that shouldn't cast any doubt on the reliability of this report. We crossed the dark, silent courtyard, past the zendo where Leonard and I sat those early mornings long ago, where Roshi married Susan and me.

I'd never been inside Roshi's little lair in the back, up a winding staircase. We entered his crowded sitting room. There was a low table on the carpeted floor and a tiny adjacent kitchen behind a beaded curtain. He was seated in a La-Z-Boy recliner, propped up on pillows. On the wall behind him there was a Japanese brushwork painting depicting Bodhidharma.

How do you explain why Bodhidharma came from the West while you are hanging from a tree branch by your teeth with a hungry tiger pacing below you?

Roshi bore a remarkable resemblance to the scowling, wild-eyed mad Zen patriarch in the painting. At 106 Roshi didn't look any older than the last time I saw him, or even the first. His eyebrows were still dark and alive like Bodhidharma's, his skin still baby smooth. It was ridiculous. Or voodoo. He stared at me, trying to place my face, but Kezban, who is very pretty, distracted him.

"Roshi quite likes her," Leonard informed me earlier. Roshi liked his inji, too, a young Japanese woman, also very pretty.

I stepped forward and bowed. Leonard and then Roshi's inji shouted in his old deaf ears: *This is Elic! Old student! Friend of Leonard! Editor of Zero! Zero magazine! Elic!*

Roshi screwed his face into a pose of extreme concentration as he wracked his memory.

"Elic?" he murmured thoughtfully. He stared at me and slapped his uncooperative head theatrically. "Memory no good." It was a heartfelt apology or a very good imitation of one. I didn't care, because the affection pouring out of his liquid brown eyes melted me as always.

"Elic!" He suddenly shook himself awake in recognition, real or feigned. Leonard was smiling. His inji was beaming. Kezban was thrilled. I was entranced.

Let the party begin!

Leonard and I sat down on the floor and tucked our crossed legs under the low table. Roshi's inji propped him up and fastened a bib under his chin, covering his impeccable pressed white robes. Kezban laid out the spread of raw fish and assorted Japanese delicacies until the table could hold no more.

Leonard gave me a sidelong glance—*See, I told you so*—as the supposedly dying man on a feeding tube wielded his chopsticks like Toscanini conducting Beethoven, like a dive-bombing hawk, like the master he was, nipping at choice morsels, pointing out the best pieces to me, even refilling my plate with a death-defying lean across the table.

"We caught him on a good day," Leonard whispered to me. Though Roshi was nearly deaf, one could never be sure.

The room was filled with joy. The captain was at the helm again, seizing the wheel, shouting orders: *Bring this, bring that, eat more, eat more!*

"Better finish it all, Old Eric, or he'll be disappointed."

I ate and ate and ate. Roshi fed me slices of raw fish like a seal at Sea World, until there was nothing left but shiso leaves. I ate those, too. Kezban and Roshi's inji cleared the table and ducked behind the beaded curtain of the kitchen. Roshi sighed deeply, paying close attention to the inner workings of his failing digestive apparatus. Leonard and I shifted our postures on the floor.

It happened very fast.

One moment we were there, or here; then we weren't. Or we were. That silly old *being and non-being* thing. The function of zero.

I'd never been in sanzen with Leonard before. You're supposed to be alone with Roshi in absolute privacy, but what the hell, we didn't have a lot of time for formalities. We were three old friends. Which doesn't imply equality. Friendship is the wordless recognition of like is like.

How do you realize true nature digesting raw fish?

∽

Leonard and I raced back to Tremaine and quickly changed into our investigative uniforms, our underwear. Despite the prodigious quantity of food so recently consumed, we were ravenous, perhaps in expectation of the long night ahead of us. We had the final piece of the puzzle in hand in the nick of time! All we had to do was fit it into place.

"There's cheese and pickles, of course, bread, half a rotisserie chicken, and some excellent chopped liver," Leonard inventoried with his head deep in the fridge. He prepared a plate of cheese and crackers for starters and opened the cabinet above the broom closet, a mysterious repository of alcohol acquired haphazardly over the years, some bottles received as gifts he'd never bothered regifting. He pulled out a bottle of absinthe and held it up for a vote. A while back he'd discovered online authentic artisanal absinthe from France delivered semi-legally to your doorstep in an unmarked international freight package. It was distilled with genuine wormwood that produced a mildly psychedelic Toulouse-Lautrec buzz. We soon acquired from the distributor traditional absinthe drinking kits: special goblets with glass funnels that you fill with ice and pour the absinthe over, creating the famous milky cloud of the green fairy who graciously transported us on several wonderful afternoons to fin de siècle Paris.

The absinthe seemed a bit louche for the rigorous investigation on the evening's agenda. We settled instead on some old Scotch, not my favorite brown liquid, but the Old Boy never developed a taste for Kentucky spirits, and it was better than vodka. We took our customary seats on each side of the table with our drinks, the plate of cheese and crackers between us like an offering on the altar. Leonard began the proceedings with his Initial Hypothesis for this Matter of Vital Interest.

"It was always just about sanzen," Leonard declared. "The rest of it was beside the point."

With a magisterial wave of his hand he dismissed our forty years of herky-jerky attempts to be monks or not be monks, our running up to Baldy and running down from Baldy, Roshi's three-ring circus of a scene, our whisperings to the world in poetry and song and novels and movies: *Psst, this is what the guy is really about*, staking out positions, various positions, and then abandoning them, one after another.

It was always just about sanzen.

Brilliant! It was concise in expression and penetrating in insight. I raised my glass to humbly toast his accomplishment. We sipped and savored.

And then we pondered, constitutionally incapable of leaving well enough alone.

I cleared my throat.

Yes?

I really didn't want to be a killjoy, but we had standards. "Um. I know we feel really good right now, but we don't feel quite as good as we did an hour ago, back there hanging out in the whole cosmos with him. Do we?"

"Not quite as good. No."

We began nibbling the crackers, then demolishing them.

We weren't done yet. Did you really think we were?

~

Some years before, I wrote a screenplay for a European TV production about the Roman Empire. I became fascinated by the murder of Julius Caesar, organized by the man whose life Caesar spared despite the man's sustained attempts to destroy him.

The man of course was Cicero.

What was it about Caesar that drove Cicero batshit?

"I must confess, Old Eric, I was always quite fond of Cicero."

"Everyone is. Every Latin student learns to admire his elegant prose, full of lofty ideals that Cicero himself never adhered to."

"Your revisions of history are breathtaking."

"Cicero was a pathetic tight-ass. A phony moralist revulsed by sex."

"And if I recollect, our boy Caesar was a notorious stick man?"

"Correct. What Caesar had, and Cicero didn't—and it was like a worm eating Cicero's brain—was . . ."

"Yes?" Leonard leaned forward, waiting for the revelation.

"*Charisma,*" I whispered theatrically. "It's the Greek word for 'the gift of the gods.'"

"How lovely." Leonard leaned back to contemplate divine largesse.

"Caesar's soldiers followed him into battle despite ridiculous odds against them. The plebs of Rome adored him. The wives of his fellow senators whom he hadn't fucked wishfully bragged that he had. Caesar possessed such a dangerous surfeit of charisma—at least in Cicero's eyes—that he threatened the very order of the mortal world."

"Cicero might have had a point there."

"Charisma makes ordinary people feel extraordinary in its presence. It makes the impossible seem possible."

"I think I know where you're going with this."

"Not just in battle. In the spiritual realm as well."

"Don't worry guys, follow me, the Red Sea is about to part!" Leonard as Moses.

We took a break to ponder this new development while we picked half a rotisserie chicken clean.

~

Roshi could effortlessly manifest true nature, Buddha nature, true self. In the presence of his radiance, your own pathetic-by-comparison limited self was obliterated.

Zap.

But was it merely charisma? That's what I was asking.

"That zap is better than anything I ever felt," Leonard noted dispassionately.

"Of course it is. It's why the followers follow the master, whether the master is Moses or Christ or Mohammed or Buddha."

"Or Charles Manson or Jim Jones pouring the Kool-Aid?" Leonard offered.

"Or Sasaki Roshi?"

Leonard raised his eyebrows. "So that's all it is, just a buzz?"

"I'm considering the possibility."

Leonard merely nodded, carefully admitting nothing except the admission of this new possibility for consideration. Only a few moments before we had the final piece of the puzzle in hand, hovering over our puzzling table, ready to fit it into place.

It was always just about sanzen.

Now it wasn't just about sanzen. It was about sanzen and sushi.

It was about *The Guy*. It always had been.

Long ago we jumped onto the spiritual path because we couldn't stand our moods. We embraced the belief that if we achieved some version of enlightenment we'd attain brand-new selves, retrofitted with a peace of mind that our factory-equipped selves-at-birth so painfully lacked. One of the most quoted exhortations of the day was from the ancient Chinese master known as the Third Patriarch of Zen:

The Great Way is not difficult for those who have no preferences.

Perfecto! Because for me and Leonard and everyone else willing and eager to sit like a statue at three in the morning, our preferences—or the much dirtier word: *desires*—were what fucked up our heads. Healthy people are unhappy a lot of the time, but it's because they can't get what they want. For us sick souls, getting what we want is as bad as not getting it. Then the Third Patriarch and Ram Dass told us that enlightenment would magically free us from the clutches of desire, and we ate that dumb shit right up!

Thus it was confusing to discover that the enlightened dudes—roshis and rinpoches and swamis and saints—possessed all kinds of desires they weren't supposed to have. We tried to comprehend the complex narratives spun to explain how even though the enlightened mind experiences desire, pain, and anger, it's different for them than for us dullards. *Attachment* is the critical component, see? Enlightened beings are not attached to the objects of their desires. They aren't even attached to their own desires!

Right from the start Roshi's American importers were simultaneously enthused by the quality of his wisdom and confused by the quantity of his shenanigans. They cabled the home temple in Japan to send over a Japanese bride to domesticate him, but she couldn't slow him down.

It's worth noting that those were different days. In pretty much every New Age spiritual scene in the sixties and seventies and even in the eighties, everyone was fucking everyone. There was little distinction between students fucking fellow students and students fucking teachers or masters. All this fucking produced more gossip than outrage at the time.

Some women wanted to engage in various levels of physical contact with Roshi. Others didn't. Some said no. Some said *no* more emphatically. As an aside, Roshi also fucked with his male students, fucking with their minds instead of their bodies. Many students left. Others stuck around because he was an otherworldly presence in the sanzen room, a powerfully charismatic critter capable of deep empathy and generosity, comforting and caring to those he liked, an utterly heartless bastard to those he didn't like, or worse, didn't respect.

Then the scandal broke.

I always thought one of the best things about Roshi's scene was that his students rarely spoke, wrote, or even muttered their own versions of what Roshi had to say. Now they did. Leonard forwarded to me daily pronouncements from many of Roshi's oldest students. They'd devoted their lives to him—never mind that he hadn't asked for the favor—and now they faced a terrible dilemma. What if with his dying breath Roshi uttered one of their names, as they'd all dreamt for decades? Would Roshi's anointed successor now want to step into the shoes of the disgraced master? How could any of them even maintain themselves as leaders of their Zen Centers in Roshi's name?

Roshi solved their problem. He lopped off their heads, dismissing, defrocking, and ridiculing virtually every one of his senior monks, both his apologists and those who wanted to clean up his act.

Cimarron Zen Center was so quiet the night we visited because there was literally no one left. A year later, he was dead. The headline in his obituary in the *New York Times* said it all: "Joshu Sasaki, 107, Tainted Zen Master."

The obituary began by characterizing him as "one of the most influential and charismatic Zen masters in America." The second paragraph noted Leonard's close connection to Roshi, as would always be the case with anything written about Roshi.

Then the juicy stuff. The obituary went into great detail recounting the unsavory allegations about Roshi that "cast his character and his legacy in a harsh light."

~

Was all of it intentional or simply clumsy execution on his part?

Leonard and I had to answer that if we still hoped to fit the final piece of the puzzle into place. He waited for me to go first.

"I don't think he ever wanted anyone to utter even a word in his name. That's why he pretended he didn't know how to speak English," I offered.

"He was quite fluent whenever he needed to be," Leonard granted.

I continued. "I don't think he ever had any interest in a 'successor.' The scandal gave him the opportunity to torch the whole thing so no one could start a religion in his name."

Leonard slowly digested my hypothesis before offering his own succinct opinion. "I don't think he gave a shit one way or another."

"Well . . ."

"I mean, he *really* didn't give a shit one way or another."

I shrugged. Were we just going to put the label: *Whatever* on the file and shove it back in the drawer? Maybe Leonard was tired and we'd exhausted our deliberations for the night. I got up to clear our plates, but he motioned for me to sit down. He put his words together carefully.

"It was always about him wanting to be the only cock in the barnyard."

"There was that."

Leonard wasn't done. "He didn't give a shit about anything anyone else did, as long as he could do what he wanted to do. He liked giving sanzen. He liked fondling girls. And he didn't like anyone telling him what to do."

"Who does?"

"My point exactly. No one does, but Roshi was the only guy I ever met who got away with it. He put together a scene where he could do exactly what he wanted to do because everyone wanted something from him. He was a total genius!"

Leonard was exuberant. It was as if he'd managed to keep this to himself all these years, waiting for the right moment to reveal it to me, and the right moment had finally come.

Are you ready, Old Eric?

Lay it on me, Old Leonard.

"Roshi has no conscience." His eyes lit up. He loved saying it aloud. "You actually figured it out. He's a hundred percent Neanderthal! It's bullshit that Roshi was some kind of self-sacrificing holy man or whatever we want holy men to be. The rest of us try to pretend we don't want what we really want, or that we're acting for some greater good. Roshi never needed to soothe his conscience because he doesn't have one."

Despite the harshness of the naked words, the tone of Leonard's pronouncement was almost wistful. What he was saying was as much about himself as it was about Roshi.

After all, you are captivated by the master because in one way or another you want to be like him, possess what you perceive to be his extraordinariness, his spiritual understanding or power that frees him from whatever you think ensnares you. What drew Leonard to Roshi from the start and what continued to entrance him was that Roshi didn't care.

He has no conscience.

But Leonard did. His conscience was woven so tightly into the fabric of his being that it was impossible for him to grab the thread and tug it out without the whole thing coming apart. Old Leo the Lion could only yearn, and wonder what his life might be like:

If I only didn't have a heart!

~

Night pivoted toward morning. I launched a last quivering arrow. "What if there's no such thing as enlightenment?"

Leonard didn't miss a beat. "Who said there was?"

"Or as your boy Balsekar used to ask: *Who cares?*"

We sure didn't. Not anymore.

Enlightenment? Ha, that's for suckas.

It had dropped out of the top one hundred hits of all time on our list of matters of vital interest, even as Roshi jumped back to the top of the charts.

"You know what he gave me, Old Eric, more than anything else?" Leonard had never expressed it this way before—what Roshi *gave* him. "Encouragement."

"Huh." It made perfect sense. Long ago Roshi encouraged him: *Cohn. Sing more sad.*

More. More. More.

Roshi gave me encouragement every time I saw him, even the very last time a year later, when we visited him a month before he died. I left encouraged.

Leonard stood behind the kitchen counter, at the pulpit, his voice rising. We were in church now for sure.

"He did something for us, Old Eric. Or to us. It wasn't just about the pleasure of his company, although that was the greatest pleasure of my life. He had some effect on me. And on you, too." He paused and waited for the right word to come to him. He practically thumped his pulpit. "He gave us confidence."

He was elated. I'd never seen him this elated and it elated me. "We're the standard-bearers," he announced.

"That's us!" I was into it now. Call and response! "We're like Job's pal, I forget his name, the one who came stumbling out of the cave shouting, 'I alone am escaped to tell thee!'"

"But we can't tell anyone!"

"Mum's the word!"

"Oooooooold Eric. What a trip!"

"Oooooooold Leonard. What a trip!"

We never felt better than we did that night in the kitchen at Tremaine, that glorious night we finally fit the final piece of the puzzle into its place even if by the next morning we'd forgotten exactly where we put it.

Six months later he called and calmly told me he'd been diagnosed with an early form of cancer. "They say it's not painful."

Leonard liked to tell set-piece jokes. This was one of his favorites. He repeated it to me several times over the years:

You ever hear the one about the guy who walks into a bank wearing a ski mask and waving a gun?

"Hands in the air, motherstickers!" he shouts with glee.

"It's a fuckup!"

eleven

VIVID SOLACE

IN JANUARY 2014, BACK at Tremaine after what was supposed to be the final show of the final tour, Leonard was considering ways to extend his idyllic life on the road. "Maybe I'll do a permanent gig at some downscale casino in Vegas. I could be the Wayne Newton of the introspective gambling set."

He had written enough new songs in hotel rooms over the past five years to record a studio album in LA while he decided what to do with the rest of his life. Then he received the diagnosis.

"It's called MDS. *Myelodysplastic syndrome*," he carefully enunciated.

I make no claim that this is an official or even entirely accurate medical account. It is true in the same way this whole story is true. It's the version Leonard and I agreed on, our consensual reality, based on what each of us knew or thought we knew and what we chose to share with each other. That's the end of the medical disclaimer.

He told me it was a bone marrow disorder that fucked up what bone marrow produces: red blood cells, white blood cells, and most importantly, *platelets*. I still don't know precisely what platelets are. We never got into details like that. What mattered was his "platelet count," a number that became our closely watched Dow Jones average for the next three years. Outside of his kids, his manager, a few close friends, and me, he didn't tell anyone he was dying. He made me promise not to tell anyone else.

"I don't exactly talk to a lot of people, y'know."

"True, but still . . ."

"Okay. Mum's the word."

"I can't deal with dying publicly."

At the outset his major symptom was fatigue. He was told that over time—two or three years, perhaps five—his falling platelet count would leave him increasingly tired, until finally, "I kind of drift away. Not such a bad way to go, eh?"

"Not at all," I concurred with only tentative enthusiasm.

"I'll speak to you later, man. I've got to get back to work."

I've recounted the insistent perfectionism Leonard always brought to his work. Nothing could rush him. Until now. He became slightly mesmerized by the grains of sand streaming through the narrow neck of the hourglass.

"It's a race to the death!" he proclaimed with caustic glee.

He teamed up with the highly credentialed producer Pat Leonard, who took Leonard's lyrics and created melodies and arrangements. Together they worked on each song until it was ready for Leonard to record, completing them at a pace Leonard had never achieved on his own before. His heart and soul were perfectly calm, but his mind had heard the news—*You're dying.*

I wanted to come down—for some reason we always called flying from Massachusetts to Los Angeles *coming down*—and hang out with him, but each time we set a date he pushed it back, pleading the necessity to get to the next stage of producing the new album. I finally got on a plane in June 2014 for a three-day trip instead of the usual week. That's how precious time had become to him.

I accompanied him to the cancer center at Cedars-Sinai Hospital in Beverly Hills where he was receiving a weekly infusion of a drug—not chemotherapy—intended to keep his platelet count up. I don't think anyone else besides Kezban went to the hospital with him, but we'd always been firsthand witnesses to the trickiest situations in each other's lives: Esther at the Mayflower, the visits he made to

Northampton when Susan was going through her hell, the times I went with him to see Suzanne in New York.

You gotta see this for yourself.

Wending our way through the hallways and elevators of the Cedars-Sinai cancer center, I recalled the time Leonard came with me to a pitch meeting. I was living in Malibu. It was only two weeks after my back surgery, but in Hollywood, like the NFL, you lie about the injury reports—the sharks and blood-in-the-water thing. I was pitching a screen adaptation of Leonard's novel *Beautiful Losers* to the Canadian director Norman Jewison, with whom I'd worked briefly before on a script.

"Why don't I come with you?" Leonard surprised me. "You know, two old Canadians?"

Jewison knew the novel of course. It's a hallucinatory tale that leaps back and forth from sixties Montreal to the seventeenth century, connected by the story of the Mohawk Indian maiden who became the Catholic saint Kateri Tekakwitha. After I finished the pitch with Leonard seated beside me, nodding his approval throughout, Jewison sighed. "I have to be honest with you. I have another Indian story on my plate." His pitch was longer than mine.

As we walked across the studio lot to the trusty red Mercedes—actually, he walked and I limped—Leonard shook his head in disbelief. "*Another Indian story on my plate?* Are you kidding me? I'm glad I got to see what you do to earn a buck. I'll drive. We need to get an ice pack for your head."

∾

I sat beside him in his comfy padded chair as he leaned back and relaxed with an infusion needle in his arm. We noted how good-looking the nurses were and wondered if they, like all the gorgeous waitresses in LA, were aspiring actresses, but that seemed unlikely, we reasoned, since they'd taken all that trouble going to nursing school. We were impressed by the democratic demographics of the cancer center at this exclusive, for-the-stars hospital, and how genuinely kind and compassionate all of the caregivers were. He introduced me to his doctor, his broker in the platelets market, a warm, concerned fellow who was enthusiastic about the positive results of the infusion treatments.

Leonard wanted to make sure we were in agreement on the terms of our discussion of this unexpected matter, placing it at an appropriate remove, a place where we could examine it and talk about it the way we talked about all important matters, not about our feelings, but what it felt like.

It ain't bad.
It feels sweet.
That's rough.
A tough one.
Brutal.

This wasn't a psychospiritual practice on our part, but an aesthetic endeavor, striking a pose for an unseen painter tucked away behind his canvas casting surreptitious approving glances at our style, the artistic rendition being more accurate to us than real life, which we considered ambiguous if not indecipherably blurry.

Leonard was committed to maintaining his pose until the end. He'd saved the best one for last, not a warrior's stance, none of that *I'll beat the big C* chest-thumping so in vogue these days, but a carefree pose that wasn't difficult for him to hold at this early stage when his symptoms were still relatively mild. He could forget about his condition for periods of time, the way pet dogs romp in the backyard until they make mindless contact with the thin electrified wire that bounds their confinement. Leonard's boundary wire was his weekly infusion at the hospital. He couldn't miss even one or bad things would happen. He couldn't get on a plane and skip town. He'd never been pinned down this way, although we'd always been constrained and bound, unable to avoid the shocking jolts of the electrified wires limiting our recreation.

He would have loved to go to Montreal, but no hospital up there had the infusion drug. He even researched packing it and taking it with him, but it wasn't possible. We considered a short road trip, renting a nifty car, not that either one of us was really a car guy, but what the hell, time to bust out and drive up the coast or out to the desert in a convertible. We never quite managed to pull it off.

Behind the drawn curtains of the cubicle, his eyes half-closed with an infusion needle in his arm, he expected that after all these years I'd understand perfectly everything he was doing without explanation, and that I wouldn't weaken, because in our terms it would be weakness, self-indulgence, to bray insulting suggestions or stupid questions, or give him moonfaced looks of sorrow and pity. It wasn't denial. It was affirmation.

After his infusion we went to lunch with Kezban at a nearby Beverly Hills restaurant. He was greeted at the door with quiet familiarity. They were once-a-week regulars, though no one knew why they came only on Mondays. As was usually the case with his favorite restaurants, the food wasn't all that good, but the ambiance was perfect. I had a Bloody Mary with my cheeseburger deluxe.

After we got back to the house we broke out the Popsicles and settled into our big chairs in front of his computer and remained there for the rest of the day listening to the tracks of his new album over and over. I loved the grooves. The lyrics were cunning and compressed. I was amazed. So was he.

The next morning I came up from the apartment in the backyard. He was already awake and back at the computer, listening, making notes to send to Pat Leonard.

I got some coffee and sat down beside him. After listening to the whole album once more, we spent the rest of the day going through his vast collection of photos, a lifetime's worth that he'd recently had digitized and stored in his computer.

"Did you ever see this one?"

"No. Who's that?"

"Me! Young Leonard!"

First a photo, then the story behind it. He wanted me to know everything about his pet dogs and the trip he took to Cuba at twenty. He wanted me to know details I'd never heard before, or had but needed to be reminded of. He wanted to fill in the blanks in my version of his life. A sweet melancholy crept into the room. We didn't mind it. In that mood we visited Roshi together for the last time that night.

On the drive over Leonard dispassionately revealed that Roshi's inji was hoarding his antibiotics, and whenever an infection flared up that might finally kill him, she blasted Roshi with a massive dose crushed up and administered through his feeding tube to stave it off.

I was a bit outraged. "What? He can't die until he names a successor? Does he know what's going on?"

"He doesn't seem to want to die." Leonard smiled, almost bemused. We'd arrived outside the gate of Cimarron.

"What's that supposed to mean?"

Sometimes Leonard displayed his flair for the dramatic. "You know what Roshi muttered to me the other day?"

I shrugged.

"Too attached to living."

"You're kidding."

"Nope. I think he was surprised himself."

We tiptoed up the staircase and quietly entered. Roshi was propped up in his recliner chair. He'd lost weight and his pallor was much duller than the last time I saw him. Roshi recognized Leonard, but he didn't have the energy to even try to remember who I was. Leonard had described Roshi's deterioration to me beforehand—two months later he'd be dead—and dismissed any possibility of a reprise of our magical sanzen ensemble of the year before. We sat on the floor as Kezban laid out the sushi on the low table, trying to arouse Roshi's interest, but his head kept dropping to his chest and his eyes closed. He made occasional dispiriting groans.

Somehow, though, he still possessed enough fierce pride to rouse himself for a Chaplinesque silent-movie rendition of his own miserable state of discomfort. He began by making exaggerated cringes and grimaces, and at the scene's comic climax he blinked his eyes in astonishment. I could practically read the caption on the silent screen: *Ain't this some shit?!*

Leonard and I smiled uncertainly, our stomachs churning. Were we supposed to applaud? We ate our sushi robotically and Roshi even managed a piece. Leonard watched him intently, making a conscious effort not to hold his breath, that intuitive, useless human attempt to stop time and prevent the next moment from exploding, as if that would keep Roshi alive a little longer. I don't know if Leonard was thinking about what his life would be like without Roshi. I had yet to start thinking about what my life would be like without Leonard, but I felt terrible that evening, and Leonard felt terrible and Roshi felt terrible. Roshi was the only one, though, who had no inhibition about letting all of us know how terrible he felt.

He was kind of disgusted with himself. Or pretended to be.

Too attached to living.

～

After our visit, Leonard didn't have to say it: *That ain't the way I want to go.*

Over the years, long before he became ill, we'd hypothetically discussed the topic. Most humans give the matter some thought. The ancient Romans were particularly concerned with "dying well," believing that how a man or woman would be remembered by posterity was of paramount import, and that one's end was the emphatic punctuation to one's life. To die a defeated captive of the enemy or humiliated by scandal was a "quality of life" issue for them. With no plug to pull you fell on your sword and were applauded for it.

Years before, Leonard pored over Kevorkian websites that recommended a combination of barbiturates and a plastic bag over your face as the most efficient, least painful exit. He intended to enlist Lorca's help if I wasn't available. We considered which of our children would step up and prove reliably unsentimental about offing their father—our daughters, definitely.

Back then we were more concerned with the means to the end rather than the specific conditions of our lives that would inspire us to end it all. We never really got around to defining the specific level of diminishment in the quality of our lives—as if the quality had ever been that great anyway—that would trigger the call to action.

In one of our first conversations after his diagnosis and prognosis, Leonard told me he'd already decided he wouldn't undergo any treatment that involved a significant degree of discomfort or hassle in order to extend his life. He ruled out bone marrow transplants, the most common procedure for his ailment, and he also took chemotherapy off the table. He was not, however, naïve. He took the soothing prediction that he would end up painlessly in bed very tired until he quietly slipped away to be just one possible scenario.

I had recently been through the difficult deaths of both my parents. "It's really easy to get into a hospital," I told Leonard. "Especially if they deliver you in an ambulance with the lights flashing. Once you call them, though, it's very hard to call the shots. They've got you."

We agreed that the one scenario to be avoided at all costs was dialing 911.

∾

"I was having too good a time, y'know," he mused ruefully.

"You were a naughty boy. Working hard every night, entertaining people and going quietly to your room alone. What an orgy of self-indulgence!"

"God forgot about me for a while. He was too busy torturing some other saps. Someone must have tipped him off: *Psst. Check out Cohen over there. He's having a ball!*"

"And now the party's over."

"Hey, I had five good years. Not a bad run."

It was a great run. Leonard had finally gained control of his life, even if it was due to the sheer luck of his manager bankrupting him. He shoved The Chauffeur out of the car, the driver who'd been driving him half-crazy his whole life, as if willfully ignoring his directions to his desired destinations. Once he finally experienced the thrill of gripping the steering wheel in his own hands, he was not about to easily relinquish it.

This is how he explained his plan to me: the infusions were prolonging his life and allowing him to do things that kept him in a good mood. He didn't feel terrible, but if he did start feeling terrible, if his condition deteriorated and his mood darkened, *if it wasn't worth the hassle,* he would stop taking the infusions and he would die. He found this comforting in an elegant way.

He canceled his plan to rent an apartment in Portland—Oregon had just passed an assisted-suicide law for legal residents of the state—tossed the hypothetical barbiturates and plastic bag in the trash, and never again mentioned his rumored hidden pistol that he supposedly kept somewhere as a last resort.

"All I have to do is not show up at the hospital one Monday morning and *sayonara.*"

～

I came up the back stairs early the next morning with my suitcase. He was already up and at his computer. "You're leaving already?" He was genuinely shocked. "You just got here."

I wasn't sure if his brain was getting addled. The night before I'd told him I had a morning plane. We'd deliberately made this a short trip.

"You don't have to go, man. I mean . . ." I don't think he was sure what he meant, except he didn't want me to go. We'd never parted this way. I felt a sudden awful sadness.

"I could change my plane." I could live in the apartment downstairs and we could have breakfast every morning and hang out and spend the rest of the day in our quarters writing and get together in the evening to talk it all over.

Why not?

"It's okay." He snapped out of it. "I'm going to New York when I finish the album. A very quick trip so I can get back for my weekly dose. But I have to appear in public or it might get out that Cohen is dying. They'd be on me like roadkill. You'll come down. It'll be horrible. We'll have a great time."

He sat beside me in the funky wooden chairs out on the front lawn until the taxi pulled up to take me to the airport.

~

I drove down from Boston on a warm, muggy mid-September afternoon a few months later and gave my car keys to the valet at the curb on 54th Street in Manhattan. The Warwick Hotel was a reasonable but by no means authentic replacement for the Mayflower, gone almost ten years by then. Leonard had booked a room for me. We were driven downtown to a hipster venue Sony Records commandeered for a "listening party" for the release of his new album, *Popular Problems.*

This was Leonard's solution to his own arcane problem. Using the clout he finally wielded over his label— none of Leonard's old nemeses at Sony survived the cratering of the record industry in the past decade, and the young crew running what was left of the company cheerfully groveled at the feet of one of the few acts whose music they could sell—he told them he'd skip the grueling grind of endless interviews he'd always done in the past to stir a breeze of interest on Sony's part in promoting a new album. Instead, he would appear exactly once in front of as many music journalists they could assemble to listen to the new album's public debut. Afterward, he'd field a few soft-toss questions, give a few witty answers, then bid them fare-thee-well-friends, leaving them to enjoy eats and drinks on Sony.

The downtown club was packed with faces in awe. I got bored halfway through and slipped out. I was about to wander into the kitchen and pounce on a magnificent tray of sandwiches when a side door to the main room swung open and I was startled, and so was she, not quite sure, but who else could it be?

"Dominique?"

"Eh-rique?"

We hadn't seen each other in almost thirty years. Her painful split with Leonard had long ago healed into a deep, abiding friendship. She'd become very close with both kids, particularly Lorca, who had an apartment in Paris for a while in connection with her antique business.

Dominique had aged into a delightful, elegant beatnik of sorts, with long, flowing gray-blond hair and serious black-framed spectacles. She was wearing an embroidered vest that I immediately complimented her on. Her whispery hoarse voice hadn't changed as she explained that she was in New York partly to help Lorca with the difficult task of cleaning out her aunt Esther's apartment and disposing of her possessions. After a long battle with cancer, Esther had died only two weeks before.

We last left Esther and Leonard and me back at the Mayflower with none of us feeling very good about our get-togethers. Maybe they had to tear the place down to change the script, but our story had an unexpectedly sweet final act. In the summer of 2006, my daughter Sara was living in New York City, doing an internship after her first year of college. Leonard was in town—this was the dismal period between dead broke and vindication—and I came down to hang out with him and provide the usual assistance with Esther. It was the first time I'd stayed at the Warwick, and it was apparent to both of us that we'd never lure her into having dinner there.

Leonard had a sudden inspiration. "We'll invite Little Sara to join us! The more the merrier." Sara had by then established her own friendship with Old Leonard, visiting him often at Tremaine, not far from her campus of USC in Los Angeles. "She's quite charming, your daughter. She speaks a bit too fast for me to understand everything she's saying, but I like listening to her anyway."

We chose the restaurant, a midtown upscale Italian place, for its walking-distance proximity to the hotel. The four of us were seated at an outdoor table, another plus. Since our days drinking Château Latour backstage at the Berklee Performance Center, my preference in wine had gone almost exclusively Italian. I suggested a bottle of Barolo.

Leonard was curious. Sara had spent a summer in Italy in high school and studied Italian since. She knew it by reputation and was eager to try it. Esther's Italian wine experience, though, was limited to wicker-clad bottles in her youth, and she was suspicious. Everything changed, however, when we touched our glasses full of the ten-year-old wine and sipped. Then we sipped again. Who knew we'd poured magic into our glasses?

"This is nice stuff, Old Eric."

"I love this wine!" Esther exclaimed.

Exclaimed!

The old-fashioned literary verb is so fitting to a tale of wonder. By the time she finished her first glass, Esther was transformed before our eyes, shedding years and tears and cares and widowhood and cancer, her hair suddenly very blond and hydrated, her eyes full of mischief, good mischief.

I perused the wine list again, encouraged by Leonard to spare no expense. He knew we were on to something. The second bottle was reverently poured and I encouraged everyone to contemplate the ring of brick red around the top of the liquid in the glass, a sure sign of the maturity and profundity of both the wine and the drinkers. Affection for her brother poured forth from Esther, and Leonard drank it up mixed with his wine. Sara realized something special was happening, even without the backstory.

"Great wine, Dad."

"Your father has a knack for these things."

"What do you call it, again?" Esther sang out in an enchanting tremolo.

"Barolo."

"Barolo."

"Ba*rr*olo," Sara corrected.

"Ba*rr*olo."

"Ba*rr*olo."

Who knows? Maybe Leonard and Esther and I would have been spared much unpleasantness if we'd only left the Mayflower restaurant—they served no Barolo there—and gone out to eat. Such speculation serves no good purpose. We referred to the occasion forever after as: *That Barolo Night with Esther.*

Now we were back at the very same restaurant, seated inside at a round table in the center of the room, where Leonard usually never cared to sit, but he didn't seem to care much about much that night, wiped out from the exertion of the cross-country trip and the public show.

Dominique was seated between us, and Leonard's manager, Robert Kory, was on the other side of him. Kezban was across the table from me. Two empty chairs awaited Lorca and a friend. They'd spent all day at Esther's apartment packing a lifetime of stuff into boxes to donate to Goodwill. Ostensibly, we'd gathered to celebrate the release of the new album, but Esther's absence was too insistent a reminder of Leonard's own precarious state of health.

He was particularly fond of the adjective *diabolical.* He used it several times to describe Esther's demise. Many rounds of chemotherapy over years had managed to tame her recurring cancer into remissions—*She's unkillable* was his amazed take on it—but in the end her body revolted against itself. She developed a very painful skin condition, a strange manifestation of the cancer. Leonard was unable to travel to her hospital bedside. Lorca made repeated trips from LA. Esther's doctors couldn't even diagnose it precisely, much less treat it. He ended up shouting at them over the phone to give his sister adequate pain medication to quell her awful discomfort.

"They're apparently concerned she'll become a junkie," he told me in bitter disgust. The disturbing confluence of their illnesses was not lost on him.

Lorca finally joined us at the restaurant table, coming straight from her aunt's apartment quite dazed and sad.

I don't think Esther ever threw anything out. Leonard could barely utter a word. He caught my eye and lifted his chin.

Hey, bro, take over, will ya?

There was nothing else to be done but order their best Barolo.

"Mmm. Nice wine."

"What's it called again?"

"Barolo."

"Man, this is tasty."

"Another bottle?"

"Let's try this one."

"This stuff is amazing!"

"And now let's try this one."

"Here's to Esther!"

"To Esther!"

Leonard wasn't supposed to drink but he sipped slowly and steadily, his body relaxing, his head moving to some inner melody in his beloved jazz waltz time. I was sucking down frequent draughts. Bebop.

Leonard declared that his plate of meatballs and spaghetti—ordered off the menu in a place like this—was cooked to perfection, perhaps the best spaghetti and meatballs he'd ever tasted. Robert Kory became a permanent convert to the cult of Barolo. Lorca seemed to have a moment of relief. Dominique kept glancing at Leonard and he at her, like an old married couple out with the kids.

∾

The next morning I could barely move. It had nothing to do with the wine. I reached for my morning dose of prednisone I'd laid out the night before on the bedside table beside a glass of water. I swallowed the pills and dropped back on my pillow waiting for the drug to kick in. Prednisone is an oral cortical steroid, an old, clumsy, effective treatment for inflammation, the drug of near last resort for asthma, which was the diagnosis I'd been carrying around intermittently since the age of five. It disappeared while I played basketball and football in high school without a wheeze, and remained in hiding for many years of pick-up playground ball and owning pet cats prohibited in my allergic youth. Then it made a comeback at fifty. I was told asthma could do that.

It had gotten a lot worse in the past couple of years. I didn't have sudden gasping attacks—I never had those—but if I got a bad cold, or it was allergy season, I felt like total shit with a throbbing headache and low-grade cough. Inhalers failed to quell the symptoms. My old primary care doc back in Northampton prescribed a "prednisone blast," a high initial dose taken for a few days before tapering off quickly. A high dose of prednisone induces an overwhelming urge to mow the lawn, clean the house, bite your nails, and cook dinner for twenty even if no one is coming over, all at the same time.

It's wonderful! Until you taper off the drug. Then it's really horrible.

Curiously, not long after his initial diagnosis, Leonard took prednisone for the first time. "Gout," he announced with wry pride. "I had no idea what the hell was going on. I thought someone snuck in the house and shot me in the toe. I'm better now."

"The prednisone worked?"

"It's terrific stuff. Better than speed. Until it makes you insane. What a nightmare."

"Told you so."

"You certainly did."

I couldn't get off the prednisone without the asthma coming back. My old doc wasn't sure what was going on. He told me to see a pulmonologist in Boston, where I'd moved by then.

My pulmonologist was a very attentive, caring guy. He was absolutely confident he could get my asthma under control. There were new and better drugs I hadn't tried yet so I tried them, but I still couldn't manage without prednisone. He called my asthma "an atypical presentation." The year 2014 ended badly for me with a pneumonia-like infection, the second in less than a year.

It turned out I didn't have asthma.

"Is this good news or bad news?" Leonard wondered.

"Depends how you look at it," I croaked, my throat swollen nearly shut from my latest infection.

"It usually does."

Despite my failure to improve for over a year, the pulmonologist didn't suggest I get a second opinion. Finally, in a feverish state I crawled into the office of a deeply thoughtful physician who concluded, after a lengthy session of questions and note taking, that I didn't have asthma and probably never did. I had chronic sinus infections.

"Now what, Old Eric?"

"Sinus surgery."

"Oh."

~

A week before my scheduled surgery, in the midst of my morning ablutions—noisy gargling and spitting up the night's phlegmy buildup—liquid seeped out of the left corner of my mouth despite my efforts to press my lips together.

A few hours later, my new primary care physician directed me to make funny faces at her. Only the right side of my face complied. The left side ignored my orders. She winced and gave me the bad news.

"I've got Bell's palsy," I reported to Leonard that afternoon

"Oh fuck, man. That's really bad. How did *that* happen?"

The nerve that controls the muscles in your face, the seventh cranial nerve, comes out of your brain in extremely close proximity to your sinus cavities. Chronic sinus infection is high on the list of causes of Bell's palsy. Aside from drooling and disfiguring your face, it can damage your eye.

"What do they do for it, Old Eric?"

"A massive dose of prednisone."

"Of course! Anything else?"

"Cross my fingers and hope it heals."

"You can still cross your fingers? That nerve isn't shot?"

"Not yet."

This was how we discussed bodily breakdowns and medical mishaps. In Leonard's world, there were very few surprises. No one else I knew really wanted to contemplate with me the regrettable chain of events that led to my facial paralysis. The conclusions were too unsettling. For us, though, avoidable disasters were an inexplicably essential component of the cosmic machinery, not the finely crafted Swiss watch of certain fans of the Higher Power, but proof to us that He has a nasty sense of humor.

What a fucking joke.

I had sinus surgery. Not a ton of fun, but my symptoms disappeared and didn't return. Even better, the Bell's palsy mostly healed. Though the muscles weren't quite strong enough for me to play the tenor sax, my longtime serious amusement, unless you looked very closely, both sides of my face pretty much matched and I didn't drool a drop. Crucial. Who wants to drink wine from a straw?

～

"God, you look worse than me," Leonard laughed as I got out of the cab from the airport in May 2015, a few months after my surgery. He was nattily dressed, waiting for me out on the front lawn, and he really did look better than me though he was supposed to be dying. "Don't worry, Old Eric. I have just the thing to fix you up."

He'd never been much for alternative medicine before. The one exception was bee pollen from a wonderful character named Bruce, a bee pollen producer from Arizona and ardent fan who showed up at Tremaine one day long ago. Recently, though, Leonard had been investigating other treatments he might partake of along with the infusions, as long as they didn't hurt.

For a while he swore by the healing power of vinegar baths—apple cider vinegar only—but even more promising, he concluded after extensive Internet research and tentative mainstream medical reports, were the positive effects on his condition from various forms of cannabis. Leonard was now a card-carrying California medical marijuana patient.

"I thought you didn't like pot?"

"I don't. I never liked what it did to my mind."

Neither did I. My mind is too busy to begin with, and I never found it effective as an analgesic. I couldn't recall us ever smoking pot together, but as I sat down in the wooden lawn chair beside him, before I'd even taken my suitcase to the guest room, he suavely whipped out a thin vape pipe from the breast pocket of his suit jacket. Of course he was an impeccable stoner. He inhaled and offered it to me.

"They've improved the technology," he assured me, whatever that meant.

We stayed stoned pretty much for the rest of the week. He had several varieties in different vape pipes, candies, and cookies, some for daytime and some for beddy-bye, whose comparative medicinal properties we intended to study scientifically, but unfortunately our methodology was rendered slipshod by the very subjects of our inquiry. Besides we were having too good a time.

It was the craziest week we ever spent together. We were on a bender. Nothing hurt. We went out on the town. We had dinner with the keyboard player from his band and his wife at an Italian steak house. We went to the movies! We'd never gone to the movies before. We went to an oyster restaurant with Adam and his wife and Leonard's grandson. We discreetly—actually, we weren't that discreet—passed the vape pipe back and forth at the table between rounds of oysters until Leonard started giggling and couldn't stop despite his efforts to swallow his giggles.

"Um, what's so funny?" I whispered, a bit concerned because Leonard wasn't what you'd call a public giggler.

"I . . . I . . . I forget," he managed before laughing out loud in massive amusement.

We were in the eye of the storm, not about to consult a radar map, a weather forecast, or even a crystal ball.

~

Not long after I got back to Boston I started feeling bolts of pain on the same side of my face where the Bell's palsy was still healing. This was strange because Bell's palsy doesn't hurt, it just paralyzes the muscles.

The other nerve in your face, the trigeminal nerve, is the sensory nerve. It tells you if a breeze is blowing or it's hot or a dentist is drilling out a tooth without Novocain. That's what it felt like down into my jaw.

"Idiopathic trigeminal neuralgia." The neurologist announced his carefully considered diagnosis after extensive blood tests and multiple MRIs had all come back "clean," revealing no proximate cause of my facial nerve going nuts. "*Idiopathic* means we don't know what's causing it, or if the pain will stop, or if it does stop whether it will come back again. There are a lot of cases like this." The neurologist made it sound straightforward. "All we can do is treat the symptoms."

The literature describes these "symptoms" as: *the most severe pain known to medicine.* In the nineteenth century it was called "the suicide ailment." Pardon me for bragging, but if you've got pain, there's something heroic in the hyperbolic. The pain was incapacitating and the drugs the neurologist gave me didn't do much for it.

"You have an atypical presentation," he told me.

I'd heard that somewhere before.

He gave me more drugs, but the pain kept getting worse, not only down my jaw but jabbing toward my eye, never-ending fireworks.

"Don't be alarmed." He actually said that to me on the phone.

A few months before, Leonard had suffered a compression fracture in the middle of his spine. He attributed it to foolishly lifting something too heavy. It took a very long time to heal. Then he had another compression fracture, and this time he hadn't lifted anything. He found out that his underlying condition, the MDS, causes a loss of bone density.

My bones are turning to dust.

Spinal fractures hurt a lot. The nerve root gets tweaked, and jolts of pain rouse the ragtag local constabulary of back muscles to freeze your body to stop tweaking the nerve. But no one can stay frozen, so you move, even if ever so gently, and the muscles locked in spasm keep jabbing the nerve root anyway.

It now seemed as if Leonard didn't really have whatever it was they'd originally told him he had—what platelets?—but some other ailment, much more problematic, whose primary symptom was exactly what his cancer wasn't supposed to do: bring him to his knees in pain.

His spine hurt much the way mine had hurt for twenty-five years. It gave us a basis for comparative commiseration. There had been unexpected congruities in our lives before, times when despite the fifteen-year disparity in our ages, our crises and our moods coincided and made us feel contemporaneous. Perhaps that's why we weren't surprised that we were not only so very ill at the same time, but we were both wrestling with excruciating pain. The only difference was our prognoses. Leonard was going to die, while I would live but might never get well. We couldn't decide who was the luckier guy.

Together in the same boat once more—vivid solace—we waved to all of them gathered on the shore, trembling with love and fear. We were relieved to get out of hailing distance. We'd lost a bit of our enthusiasm for reassuring them as we always had that everything would be all right.

For so much of our lives, females, women, girls, *chicks*—yes, that was the word he used most in all its rich affection, awe, and frustration—dominated our phenomenal worlds, that is, *our worlds of phenomena*. They were the background and foreground, the reference points and inspirations for so many plans and schemes and dreams and nightmares. Now it was pain instead of girls.

A 1–10 pain scale, if used correctly—if you correlate the number to an activity rather than a sensation, 7 indicating that you can't get out of a chair rather than *it's stabbing* or *it really hurts a lot*—can help you decide how to treat the pain. However, the number on the scale says nothing about one's own particular tolerance for pain. What number is too much for *you?* What number is the point at which you really want to know, as Leonard often asked: *How much can a guy stand?*

We trudged alongside one another into uncharted regions in search of the limits of our tolerance for un-remitting, off-the-scale physical pain. We were no longer searching for enlightenment, rebirth, awakening, or re-lease. Only relief. And we couldn't find it.

Our old friend Richard Cohen quoted J. M. Coetzee, a favorite author of all three of us: *Pain is truth; all else is sub-ject to doubt.*

~

"You've got to go see him now." I heard Jennifer's voice through the thick blanket around my brain, like the in-sulation sprayed into attics, the product of the cocktail of antiseizure meds and tranquilizers my neurologist pre-scribed, whose only effect was to render me hypnotically suggestible to his ridiculous assurance: *Don't be alarmed.*

"You'll feel awful if you don't see him again before he dies." Jennifer stood at the edge of the bed where I was curled up in my darkened room.

It was September 2015. I'd already had a few scares when I didn't hear from him for a couple of days. I managed to crawl onto a plane to LA.

~

"I almost called last night to tell you to put it off." He made no effort to rise from the wooden lawn chair. We watched the cab from the airport pull away.

"I'm glad you didn't."

"Yeah. Me, too." He grimaced as he shifted his weight, down quite a bit since the last time I saw him. The nails on the rickety chair seemed to be working their way dangerously free. I lowered myself gingerly into the chair beside him. To add insult to injury, my old spinal problem was sizzling because I couldn't maintain any regular exercise.

"Good to see you, bro." He exhaled slowly. "Let's not move for a moment or two, eh?"

"Brilliant."

We didn't move much for the next six days. We left the house only once, for his weekly infusion. Kezban kept the refrigerator full. Lorca, very pregnant with her second kid, magically produced some glorious take-out dinners, which we all partook of at the picnic table on the front lawn. The backyard had somehow become the front yard after all these years.

Inside, we mostly sat in the living room. The small, hard antique chairs at our sacred kitchen table had become too

inhospitable for our screaming nerves. We took turns lying on the couch or slouching in the padded, enveloping
armchairs. The low table between us was covered with our
combined stashes laid out for inspection, consideration,
and experimentation. We were grumpy and, in our estimation, undermedicated.

"Let's see." Leonard peered through his glasses. It was
early in the day and he was still in his underwear, practical
garb for trying out his latest prescription, fentanyl patches.
He carefully peeled off the backing on one of them. "I had
to promise my doctor I wouldn't squirrel the narcotics he
parses out to me in uselessly inadequate doses and take
them all at once." Leonard carefully pressed his patch into
place on his skinny bicep. "Michael Jackson really fucked
up the scene for everyone around here."

"I have all the opioids I want," I noted dispassionately.
"But they don't seem to influence my trigeminal nerve's
complaint."

"I can't imagine that pain. It's right next to your brain."

"Seems to be inside. A home invasion."

"Maybe if you put one of these patches on your face it
would help. What have you got to lose?" He laughed, then
quickly tried to stifle it. "Fuck, it hurts when I laugh."

"Me, too."

"It ain't so funny."

But that wasn't going to stop us. We told jokes all week
and made believe we didn't notice that no one else was

laughing. Old Richard Cohen dropped by a few times and tried to hide his alarm at our grim, contorted faces.

Leonard examined other possibilities on the coffee table. "Maybe a little hash brownie? What do you think?"

We managed to mix and match and take enough so that we could crawl into the kitchen late one night for a proper inquiry into this latest development.

"What are you going to do?" I asked him.

Alone in my dark bedroom back home, curled up in my private agony, I had imagined, in an almost hallucinatory way, Leonard sitting in his chair out on the front lawn on a Monday morning when he should have been at the hospital for his weekly infusion.

Was it time?

He'd waited to tell me until I managed to get here, for us to take our places at the kitchen table, no matter how uncomfortable.

"I don't want to die." He lowered his voice. This was strictly confidential. "I know. I'm as surprised as you are to find this out."

The drugs and the pain slowed my reaction. Like the movement of tectonic plates, it took a while for continents to collide.

"This won't go on forever, naturally." He nodded as if to reassure himself of that. "But I'm not going to end it."

I understood completely and not at all.

∼

A few months later, an eminent neurosurgeon at Massachusetts General Hospital showed me on his computer screen one of the supposedly "clean" MRIs taken months before that had revealed no cause of my trigeminal neuralgia.

"Here's the good side." He pointed to the spot he wanted me to look at. "The trigeminal nerve and the adjacent blood vessels are supposed to look like this. Now look at the left side. It doesn't look the same, does it?"

From where I was sitting six feet away, it looked like a multiple car crash, the blood vessels and nerve a nasty tangle.

The neurosurgeon didn't hide his irritation. Three radiologists had read three different MRIs and missed it. My symptoms of severe and rapidly increasing pain, he told me, couldn't possibly be caused by anything but the blood vessels compressing the nerve. That's why the drugs were doing nothing for the pain. My neurologist should have sent me to the neurosurgeon immediately, long before I finally managed to find him by myself.

He told me he'd done a thousand procedures to fix this and urged me to have surgery as quickly as possible. A week later, in December 2015, he drilled a hole about the size of a quarter in my skull behind my ear and put tiny, soft spacers around the three blood vessels pressing against the nerve. He packed up the hole with some nifty cement made of powdered bone and adhesive and sewed up the long incision in the skin from near the top of my skull down to my neck.

I sent Leonard a picture. I don't take many selfies, but this one was too good to pass up.

He quickly called me. "Good grief! You look like you entered a Russian saber-dueling tournament. And came in second."

It took several months to recover from the surgery and get off all the drugs. Then the pain returned. It was nearly as bad as before. The neurosurgeon wasn't thrilled, but he told me this had always been a possibility because the injury to the nerve was severe. He was confident, however, that it would fully heal in time.

"How long?"

"Nerves heal very slowly. It could take a year. Or two."

It took that long, but I'm okay now. At least my fifth and seventh cranial nerves are okay.

twelve

MATTERS OF
VITAL INTEREST

We had to keep working.

It was our most reliable source of pain relief, the only thing the two writers were not ambivalent about.

He called it: *Blackening the page.*

I called it: *Scribbling.*

Over the years, we talked about it with the kind of enthusiasm that hunting trips, weekend sports leagues, or even sex can arouse in guys.

"I never have to force myself to pick up the notebook. I have to force myself to do everything else," I noted.

"We're just a couple of junkies."

"At least we managed to get away with it."

"I get up in the morning and there's this moment of quiet uncertainty until I've got the first mug of coffee in hand and I grasp the knob on one of those old radios with the tubes and the cloth grill and move the tuner back and forth through the static and the chatter, patiently hoping I'll tune it in."

"The voice?" I asked.

"Oh, what blessed relief each time I hear it."

"I feel as if I'm taking dictation from that voice."

"I think the old guys called her *The Muse.*"

"Not the girl sleeping beside you."

"I can't sleep with a girl beside me. I don't know how you do it, Old Eric."

Sometimes we called each other merely to recount a particularly exquisite episode.

"I was in the backyard and the sun was shining, but it wasn't too hot. I'd taken a half tab of speed with my coffee, and I had my notebook on my knee. What more could a guy want?"

"It was five a.m. and the words were flowing down my arm as I watched the pen move across the page."

But as the pain got worse, it became harder and harder to write.

Are you still writing? we asked each other frequently, hopefully.

I'd developed a brutal regime. I held off on my morning dose of pain meds and made my way carefully from bed downstairs to the reclining chair I wrote in, stopping along the way to make coffee, trying not to move my head lest I rouse the sleeping serpent and feel its breath of fire inside my face, managing an hour, sometimes two, neck aching from holding my head still.

"You lucky boy. Two hours."

He wrote in the middle of the night when his pain was at its ebb. "I keep my notebook beside the bed. The days are hell. If I'm lucky I sleep a lot." Sometimes what he was writing made no sense, like Scrabble. "I think I've been writing the same page every day."

"Writing is torture. Not writing is intolerable."

"That captures it nicely."

One day, out of the blue he announced, "I may be writing songs. I almost have enough for an album."

"You're kidding."

"What else is there to do? I even have a title. *You Want It Darker.*"

"Catchy."

"It's not bad. I have no idea if I can record it. I don't think I can get out to the studio in the backyard, much less sing. What are you working on, Old Eric?"

"I seem to be writing about Roshi."

"Always a fascinating subject."

I hesitated. "And me."

"An even more fascinating subject."

"And you. It's our story. Our investigations of the past forty years. The riffs."

"That's what you do best."

"Thanks, man."

I heard a long, appreciative sigh. "I'm very glad to hear about this development. Let me read it when you're done."

"Of course."

~

In a sense the most important element of our lifelong conversation—stringing one pearl of discovery after another on the fragile necklace of our understanding—even more important than the subject under discussion or the conclusions we arrived at, was the tone we listened for in each other's voices, the tone that reassured us of our essential agreement. The tone was heartfelt about our lives yet heart-less, funny but *it's no joke, man*, even though it was! It was a fucking joke! The joke was on us of course, but not too bitter, spicy rather, a tone of irony, if you can appreciate the irony in these things, which of course we did, at least most of the time.

We pitched our voices to our special tuning fork to get it right.

Without knowing it, we'd been practicing all those years for this.

After my brain surgery in December 2015, I had a brief respite from the worst of the symptoms and I was eager to get on a plane for LA. Then the pain returned, and we were both going downhill with alarming velocity. Finally, without having to say it, we knew it was unlikely we'd ever see each other again, get to look each other in the eye as we listened closely to the tone of our lives.

It became harder and harder for him to even talk on the phone without coughing and painfully rattling his fractured vertebrae. We'd try to find a good day, a good hour, when he was strong enough to speak more than a few words. Finally he told me, in the terse manner of certain admissions we sometimes made to each other, that he didn't want to just talk about how rotten we felt. We had standards to maintain.

Email was the only medium left to us for extemporizing, philosophizing, and entertaining each other. Text messages were too confining. However, the tone of an email can easily be misconstrued, or maybe it's just the tone of my emails. Leonard was better at it than me. In the past his emails had been mostly brief informational bulletins between visits and phone calls, but they were compressed and sparse and never failed to hit the essential chord of our tone.

Maintaining this tone was more essential than ever as the stakes rose and we reported to each other on our quests—as if we'd set forth from opposite sides of the forest, the West Coast and the East Coast—in search of the Holy Grail: a serviceable drug to ease our physical pain, a med whose ancillary properties weren't worse than the pain itself.

For a while his fentanyl patches managed to take the edge off the knifelike, cross-eyed sensation caused by his fractured vertebrae. Then he wrote to me that the drug made his feet swell so badly he had trouble putting his shoes on. He made the description of his predicament sound as if he were muttering to himself in an old black-and-white sitcom.

I had the perfect solution to the problem: *Maybe put patch on feet.*

He replied that if he put the patch on his feet, his head would swell and he couldn't get into his hat.

Good one, Old Boy.

What I was taking had different but no less unpleasant side effects. The standard pain med for a screaming trigeminal nerve is some version of Neurontin, originally an antiseizure drug, now aggressively marketed on TV in its new incarnation, Lyrica, the cure for whatever ails you.

One morning he greeted me oddly in his email, asking how I was doing, addressing me as: *fellow Bdhist.* We'd never referred to each other before as Buddhists.

What was up with that?

Aha! He was tossing me a set-up line for a bracing rant!

My fingers quickly tapped the keys like an Old West Morse-code telegrapher inside a desperate fort besieged by justifiably hostile indigenous people.

The doctors lie. Then they lie more when they get it wrong. And the Buddhists are the biggest liars of all. I have no idea why

I gave up on dope and asked my doctor for this stupid drug. "No side effects," he assured me. Right. I had no idea he was a Buddhist. Now I'm on enough meds to tranc an elephant. I can't walk around the block, much less drive a car. If I wanted to. Or move from this chair. How bout you old boy?

At least I could sit in a chair. He'd recently suffered another compression fracture and reluctantly submitted to nerve blocks. Then he got talked into a weird procedure—kyphoplasty—injecting cement into his disintegrating vertebrae.

I told him I might try injecting cement into my face.

∾

Even so, there were unexpected respites.

He described a lovely night and the insights it inspired, along with *several bogus brands of surrender.*

It didn't last. Opioids completely wrecked his gut, finally putting him into the hospital. He sent me a selfie from his hospital bed with his doctor posed beside him, and in the caption he wondered why his doctor looked so happy.

Out of the hospital and back at Tremaine, he made the decision to get off all the pain meds. He went cold turkey and white-knuckled it through opioid withdrawal. He had no appetite and he was losing weight alarmingly. He noted that no one seemed to know what to do, which he found very reassuring. He wanted to know, as always, how I was doing.

I get three hours in the morning where I'm conscious and in low pain like now, taking precious moments to file this report, then the drugs hit and no good thoughts. Not a one and prognosis is . . . what prognosis? I know an opium den in Penang. Might still be there 50 years later. Let's go there and die.

He was thrilled by my proposal. At last I'd come up with a good idea!

I asked him if he could even get out of the house because I barely could.

We'd always had very different relationships to sunshine. Over the years, hanging out in our tiny backyard in various dilapidated chairs, I would edge toward the shade of the citrus trees or the house itself, while Leonard luxuriated in the intense Southern California sunshine licking his arms and face, contented as a cat, murmuring how much better this was than the land of his youth.

"Montreal was so fucking cold, man."

Sometimes we sat on his back porch upstairs off the bedroom, where I could lean back under the awning while he pulled his chair up to catch every ray of the afternoon sun slowly dropping into the Pacific Ocean ten miles to the west.

At the end, though, he preferred the small porch outside his front door at the top of the stairs. It was not much more than a landing, but over the years pots of plants filled a small table beside which he'd now sit in a suit and tie, surveying the street below.

He wrote to me that he'd been trying all morning to get out of bed and take the few steps necessary to get to his little porch, but he wasn't sure if he would make it that day. In a few brief lines, a self-portrait in black-and-white, a pose of course, a stance of noncommittal wonder, he recalled that a long time ago he'd come to LA for the sun.

Or was it Roshi?

~

He sent me another photo of himself, lying in his bed on his back with his head propped up on a pillow, wearing a hat and big headphones and his oversized glasses. His eyes are closed, a look of intense concentration on his face, and one hand is raised as if he's conducting the music coming from the iPhone he's holding in his other hand. He captioned it: *Pretending to hang in there.*

~

I was momentarily out of pain right after my surgery in late 2015, and it seemed like I'd dodged another bullet, so Jennifer and I booked a trip to Rome to celebrate. By the time we got there in May 2016, the pain had returned full force, and we weren't able to do much except take walks in the city's great public parks. Even so it was a respite.

"We should retire to Italy," Jennifer announced one day as we sat on a bench in the Borghese gardens. It was a brilliant inspiration. We quickly did the calculations. We could sell our house and move to Italy in three years.

Leonard thoroughly approved.

He knocked out a poem to celebrate our plan about the tradition of retiring to Italy, though he forgot exactly which tradition it was, informing me, in case I didn't know, that the English poets had once retired to Italy, and then English homosexuals, until all the English went to Spain instead, leaving Italy as the retirement destination of choice for writers and doctors, praising me for getting out of Dodge, and promising to visit me in Italy on his way to Hydra, where he intended to retire himself.

The renewed pain in my trigeminal nerve got so bad I had to go back on the horrible drugs. At the same time, Leonard's condition reached a tipping point. Up until then his resolve not to consider, much less pursue, any hastening of his demise had yet to be challenged. He hadn't reached the limit of his tolerance. He even managed to record the new album in his living room, an astounding project that his son ended up producing. He told me that Adam had saved his ass.

Of course working together drove them slightly bonkers, but it was an unexpected late gift for both of them from the powers that be, the last gift Leonard would receive. By the time the album was finished, his pain was nearly unendurable, and the longer he endured it, the worse it got. It was as if he now heard a cruel taunting whisper in his ear: *Oh, you want to live, is that what you said, asshole? Try living through this!*

His mood darkened in a way I'd never known before. He drew away, as if sensing how poisonous his mind had become, and he didn't want to infect me. It was an act of kindness, but I couldn't bear him taking even half a step back. It suddenly felt as if he'd already died. I couldn't stand it, and I reminded him of our rallying cry:

Stay in close touch!

It took only one reminder.

We were tough guys, remember?

That was an essential note in our tone, the seventh of the chord, but now we had only words on virtual paper to portray those tough guys.

Old Leonard. We've long talked of a lack of interest in things, everything. This feels complete. It feels like I ought to be checking out. But I have this very strong feeling that my feelings in the matter are irrelevant. That staying alive is not under the list of things the mind decides, like breathing or blood circulating or bowels moving. That's what we do, as long as the mind is reasonably functional—and you've been cursed with a reasonably functioning mind—you stay alive. I feel rather stunned by this latest revelation.

He thought I'd hit the nail on the head regarding this most vital matter of interest: *the decision to stay or leave.* He was in terrible shape. His fractures weren't healing and there was no relief from the pain. He confided that even though he was still determined not to do anything about it for the time being, some kind of spontaneous request to the Authority was now voicing itself in his mind: *to take him while he was sleeping.*

This raw honesty made it feel as if he were actually in the room with me, as if I were turning to him at the bar of the Mayflower to tell him:

I had a really good thought about an hour ago for this thing I'm writing. But I couldn't get my hand to move the pen. Staring into space while the impulses are trying to leap across the synapses— the Neurontin inhibits them, so you don't have a seizure—in this pause I'm thinking, maybe there's some insight that has been hidden from me all these years and now and now and now and now and now and now and now and now

He exclaimed: *Holy shit,* but modified his use of *holy,* noting that *holy* and *delusional* could be synonymous in the strange realm we'd been driven into by the pain. He wanted me to know that even though it doesn't help that much, only now and then, I wasn't alone.

∽

It's all your fault, I wrote. *I have no problem blaming a dying man. Obviously God wanted you to have some company in your final misery. The only way you can make this up to me is to take me with you. I just noticed that my ticket is a round trip, but maybe the conductor won't notice if I slip off with you at the last stop and don't get on for the return.*

He replied that he'd make sure they let me off the train.

~

Grim here, I began. *I seem to be left with some permanent nerve damage. Longer it goes, less likely to heal. Pain waxes and wanes from annoying to incapacitating. The effect of the constant neural assault is a deep isolation, nothing I've ever experienced. No end in sight. The rest of me is in tauntingly excellent health. Strange bitterness has seeped in, maybe been seeping for a while. I'm not myself, but then, who is? Even getting tired of my own cleverness. Hope your ordeal is a bit more gentle.*

  old eric

~

He was trying to finish a collection of poems, mostly out of boredom, he said. He described to me the experience of waiting to die. He vigilantly kept the truth of his condition a closely guarded secret. He said people wanted to visit because they thought he was convalescing and could use the company. He described the brutal details of his deterioration more graphically than ever. The ironic tough guy faltered momentarily. I could almost hear his tormented moan, coming clean with the stark truth that his ordeal was taking much too long. And then he thanked me, suddenly and expectedly, because my bitch had given him permission to spit out his own bitch, which, he informed me with a touch of pride, he rarely expressed to anyone.

I really appreciate that, old Eric.

My hands were shaking as I typed a reply: *We've always bitched to each other and kept it from the rest of them.*

Sara moved to Sweden in the spring of 2016 with no plan to return. She wanted to become an expat and get out of Dodge. She got a good job over there and bought an apartment in Stockholm. She knew it was a blow to me, but she'd hung in close during my entire ordeal, and now she didn't want to hear me wail: *Don't go!* I bit my lip. It didn't even hurt, one good effect of the nerve-numbing drugs I was on. Despite my coma-like mood, and the dismal uncertainty of whether the pain would ever relent, Jennifer and I made a trip to visit Sara in September 2016.

Leonard was amazed I'd undertake such a journey in my condition.

We're leaving this evening, I emailed him. *Meet me there? I have a lot of Percocets. We can swallow them all and jump off one of Stockholm's supposedly scenic bridges.*

He was very excited. He wrote that he would indeed meet me there, near the place where they sell good herring.

When I got to Stockholm, I sent him a picture of me standing on a bridge and wrote: *This looks like a good one to jump off.*

I was still standing on the bridge when I got his quick reply. He claimed that it was the same bridge near his hotel long ago, the one he'd jumped off many times, but only died a few times.

~

We discussed his taking up smoking cigarettes again. Not exactly life threatening anymore. I asked him if he thought it was time, and he sent me a photo that Adam had taken of the Old Hipster on the little porch outside the front door at Tremaine, wearing a brimmed hat, leaning on the railing with a lit cigarette dangling from his fingers.

~

As he trudged deeper and deeper into no-man's-land, he wanted me to accompany him as far as I could go. It wasn't about bravery or equanimity. It wasn't about fuck-all except that we were the best of friends. We didn't want to part until we absolutely had to. We wanted to keep the conversation going for as long as we could manage it.

Happy Day of the Dead! I saluted him. It was one of his favorite holidays. It was the first week of November. I went on:

We should have lit out for Mexico a long time ago where they really know how to have a good time. I went to my grandson's

second birthday party Sunday. My son and his wife and their
friends with all their kids. Young healthy thirty year old guys with
glazed dazed eyes sunk in their chairs. Ghosts already. The wide
hipped women upright and smug. They don't just run the scene,
they are the scene. The only game in town. Which we played rather
badly you and I, singing our tunes and telling our tales. Like
Macbeth while the Lady took care of business. Speaking of ghosts,
both my ex wives and my old girlfriend visited me in my dreams
last night in various states of undress. Jennifer was there too,
rather bored with it all.

   Happy Day of the Dead!

He complimented me on a great piece of reporting before describing matter-of-factly some kind of corner he'd
turned that had left him without appetite for food, or the
ability to stand up for very long, or even the desire to get
out of bed. He found it refreshing.

   maybe maybe at last

~

I visited Leonard in Montreal in 1984 and we went sight-
seeing. We visited his boyhood house in the neighborhood
of Westmount and toured the historic old city down at the
waterfront. We drove out to the Indian reservation and
bought souvenirs of Saint Catherine Tekakwitha, the her-
oine of *Beautiful Losers*. We drove up Mount Royal to the
Jewish cemetery and paid our respects at the Cohen family plot.

A few weeks before he died he sent me a photo of the neatly tended graves of his forbears that he entitled: *Family Gathering*.

I stood beside those graves on November 10, 2016, a chilly gray day as so many are in Montreal. A yawning hole awaited the elegant, plain pine casket containing Leonard's body. He'd insisted that his funeral be very small, not even a funeral at all, whatever that meant.

There were only a few of us: Adam and his wife and son; Lorca and her two children; his manager, Robert Kory; Kezban; his childhood friend Mort; Hazel—*Hazie, you dear creature*—who'd lived in one of the adjoining houses on Rue Vaillières in Montreal for as long as I'd known him; Dominique, his most cherished visitor in his last months; and me. We were not merely grief-stricken, but against all reason we were stunned. We couldn't believe he was gone.

The day began in uncertainty as to how we should follow his wishes and put him into the ground without a funeral. Thankfully, Lorca and Dominique improvised a minimalist finale. The rabbi from his Montreal temple recited a brief prayer, and then, before kaddish, I spoke.

I wanted to tell Adam and Lorca something as we gathered beside the deep, impatient hole about to swallow their father's body.

Throughout his ordeal without a whisper of complaint Leonard had maintained his impeccable posture as the father who was always there for his kids with a sympathetic ear and a shoulder of comfort. It was, of course, a brilliant defensive posture as well, a bulwark against the profound disappointment of not receiving what you might ask for from your children. It factored into his resolution to live no matter the terms. He was determined to play his role until the very end and never have to ask his children: *Let me go.*

He didn't. But in his final weeks the deterioration of his body drove his mind into a hell he never could have imagined. He couldn't let them in the door because he couldn't bear for his children to experience him as anything less than the delighted and delightful father they'd always known.

Nothing hurt more because he knew how much it was hurting them. But he couldn't help it. He was helpless.

I knew that place, where physical pain pries you apart and separates heart and flesh from the curious plasma we call mind. You cede your mind to the pain, make any desperate deal you can negotiate, tell them anything they want to know, make it up if you must. You have nothing left to betray.

Humiliated, you can't face anyone. You can't straighten up and fly right and the last thing in the world you can do is reassure your kids that everything will be okay. You can't stand their fear and you can't stand the sorrow you're causing them. He told me all of that. He wanted me to tell it to his kids because he couldn't.

Gathered around his open grave, I stared at the pine box and the close gray sky over Mount Royal, and then I told them that Old Leonard and Old Eric spent forty years considering our matters of vital interest, and each time we exhausted our speculations, we concluded by asking: *So how are the kids?*

I told them that being *Leonard Cohen* never much mattered to him compared to being their father. I told them that nothing affected his mood, nothing lifted his spirits or darkened his day the way their fortunes and struggles and stabs at happiness moved him.

"He told me more than once that on his gravestone they should just put: *Father.*"

$\sim$

That night we sat at a long table in the far corner of Moishes, the old-fashioned steak house around the corner from his house on Rue Vaillières. We kept looking over our shoulders at the door, wondering when he was going to join us. We drank Barolo of course. His death had still not been announced publicly in order to keep his funeral private. Now it was time to tell the world.

The next morning, in the cab on the way to the airport, the events of the past day started to settle in my mind into a narrative.

Wait until Old Leonard hears this.

~

Four days earlier I was up and working at five a.m. It was the middle of the night in LA, but I emailed him anyway, figuring I'd get in a few hours of writing before he woke up and replied. I was feeling good. The surgeon's prediction of recovery finally seemed to be coming true. The worst of the pain was starting to recede, and Jennifer and I revived our plan to retire in Italy. We'd even started learning Italian. I told Leonard the good news.

I was surprised when I got this reply at three thirty in the morning his time:

> *Per me si va ne la città dolente,*
> *per me si va ne l'etterno dolore,*
> *per me si va tra la perduta gente.*

I was elated. He still had the wit and energy to quote Dante's *Inferno* in Italian off the cuff at three in the morning! He was still *Old Leonard*! The knot of dread that had been clogging my chest for the past few weeks instantly dissolved while I looked up the translation:

> *Through me the way into the suffering city,*
> *Through me the way to the eternal pain,*
> *Through me the way among the lost.*

Brilliant!

Before I could reply, though, another email appeared in my inbox. In clear, grim prose he recounted how he'd gotten up to go to the bathroom, and on his way back he fainted and took a hard fall, hitting his head on the floor. It was a struggle, he said, but he'd managed to crawl back into his bed and tap out this email to me.

Dread returned so quickly that my mind went blank, unable to find words of comfort. I made a desperate joke, a useless stab at humor, asking him if the back door was open so he could make his way out to the porch and jump, but maybe it wasn't high enough to finish him off. Even as I sent it I felt our thin armor of humor dissolve.

I sat numbly staring at the screen waiting for more words from him.

Another email finally arrived, describing how sweet it was to be back in his bed, telling me that the waves of sweetness felt overwhelming. My eyes welled up with tears of relief and gratitude and most of all amazement.

I wrote that I was amazed how he was seeing this ordeal through to the end.

But I wasn't ready to send it. There was something else I needed to add, something more I needed from him, a re-assurance only he could give, and so I wrote: *I wonder if I'll have that kind of strength at the end?*

I hit send and suddenly I was standing in his doorway between the kitchen and the bedroom upstairs at the house on Tremaine.

He waved from his bed and said that if it came this way for me, the way he felt right now, it was very sweet.

He was telling me it would all be fine.

I asked him if it was very quiet and he said it was. Nothing was broken and the residue of sweetness, he said, was still with him.

I stepped closer to the bed. I looked at him lying there peacefully. I was looking at my entire life.

I backed out of the doorway and returned to my chair in my basement writing room three thousand miles away where another email from him was waiting for me, telling me that this had been quite a little excursion, and he was glad I'd been there with him.

I could no longer hold back the tears as I wrote: *We've had quite a few little excursions in our time, Old Boy. As you've often said: What a trip.*

I sent it to him and waited.

Almost an hour went by. I didn't move. I could feel the sun coming up behind me through the window, the morning light creeping into my workroom. Then his final report arrived, still lucid, describing how the full effect of his fall had finally hit him, overwhelming him, ending him.

I wrote back quickly, desperately, several times, but there was no reply.

Our long conversation had finally come to an end.

ACKNOWLEDGMENTS

IN LEONARD'S ABSENCE, MY dear friend Laura Munder helped me find the right notes.

Chris Fiore, my high school English teacher, read my first short story some fifty years ago and told me how to make it better. I read the early chapters of this book to him shortly before he died. He was in a nursing home, blind, bound to a wheelchair by Parkinson's, but his mind was as sharp as ever. He told me how to make it better.

Catherine Blinder came up with the working title, *Vivid Solace,* and started the book on its way to publication.

Mark Kramer, writer and teacher, read the proposal and helped me define the book.

Geri Thoma is the most wonderful agent I've ever worked with.

Ben Schafer, my editor at DaCapo, is a light-handed wizard whose total confidence in the enterprise was invaluable to me.

My wife, Jennifer, who lived with me through some of the most difficult parts of the story and the writing, has my love and gratitude.